The Kentucky Bicentennial Bookshelf
Sponsored by

KENTUCKY HISTORICAL EVENTS CELEBRATION COMMISSION

KENTUCKY FEDERATION OF WOMEN'S CLUBS

and Contributing Sponsors

AMERICAN FEDERAL SAVINGS & LOAN ASSOCIATION

ARMCO STEEL CORPORATION, ASHLAND WORKS

A. ARNOLD & SON TRANSFER & STORAGE CO., INC. / ASHLAND OIL, INC.

BAILEY MINING COMPANY, BYPRO, KENTUCKY / BEGLEY DRUG COMPANY

J. WINSTON COLEMAN, JR. / CONVENIENT INDUSTRIES OF AMERICA, INC.

IN MEMORY OF MR. AND MRS. J. SHERMAN COOPER BY THEIR CHILDREN

CORNING GLASS WORKS FOUNDATION / MRS. CLORA CORRELL

THE COURIER-JOURNAL AND THE LOUISVILLE TIMES

COVINGTON TRUST & BANKING COMPANY

MR. AND MRS. GEORGE P. CROUNSE / GEORGE E. EVANS, JR.

FARMERS BANK & CAPITAL TRUST COMPANY / FISHER-PRICE TOYS, MURRAY

MARY PAULINE FOX, M.D., IN HONOR OF CHLOE GIFFORD

MARY A. HALL, M.D., IN HONOR OF PAT LEE,

JANICE HALL & MARY ANN FAULKNER

OSCAR HORNSBY INC. / OFFICE PRODUCTS DIVISION IBM CORPORATION

JERRY'S RESTAURANTS / ROBERT B. JEWELL

LEE S. JONES / KENTUCKIANA GIRL SCOUT COUNCIL

KENTUCKY BANKERS ASSOCIATION / KENTUCKY COAL ASSOCIATION, INC.

THE KENTUCKY JOCKEY CLUB, INC. / THE LEXINGTON WOMAN'S CLUB

LINCOLN INCOME LIFE INSURANCE COMPANY

LORILLARD A DIVISION OF LOEW'S THEATRES, INC.

METROPOLITAN WOMAN'S CLUB OF LEXINGTON / BETTY HAGGIN MOLLOY

MUTUAL FEDERAL SAVINGS & LOAN ASSOCIATION

NATIONAL INDUSTRIES, INC. / RAND MCNALLY & COMPANY

PHILIP MORRIS, INCORPORATED / MRS. VICTOR SAMS

SHELL OIL COMPANY, LOUISVILLE

SOUTH CENTRAL BELL TELEPHONE COMPANY

SOUTHERN BELLE DAIRY CO. INC.

STANDARD OIL COMPANY (KENTUCKY)

STANDARD PRINTING CO., H. M. KESSLER, PRESIDENT

STATE BANK & TRUST COMPANY, RICHMOND

THOMAS INDUSTRIES INC. / TIP TOP COAL CO., INC.

MARY L. WISS, M.D. / YOUNGER WOMAN'S CLUB OF ST. MATTHEWS

The
Three Kentucky
Presidents

Lincoln, Taylor, Davis

HOLMAN HAMILTON

THE UNIVERSITY PRESS OF KENTUCKY

Research for The Kentucky Bicentennial Bookshelf
is assisted by a grant from the
National Endowment for the Humanities.
Views expressed in the Bookshelf do not
necessarily represent those of the Endowment.

ISBN: 0-8131-0246-4

Library of Congress Catalog Card Number: 77-92922

A statewide cooperative scholarly publishing agency
serving Berea College, Centre College of Kentucky,
Eastern Kentucky University, The Filson Club,
Georgetown College, Kentucky Historical Society,
Kentucky State University, Morehead State University,
Murray State University, Northern Kentucky University,
Transylvania University, University of Kentucky,
University of Louisville, and Western Kentucky University.

Editorial and Sales Offices: Lexington, Kentucky 40506

To the memory of Frank Roberts,
Indiana newspaperman and wonderful friend

Contents

Acknowledgments

THE AUTHOR WISHES to express his thanks for ideas, expertise, and scholarly aid of various kinds to Charles P. Roland, Alumni Professor of History at the University of Kentucky, Lexington; to Frank E. Vandiver, provost of Rice University, Houston, Texas; and to Mark E. Neely, Jr., director of the Louis A. Warren Lincoln Library and Museum, Fort Wayne, Indiana. Other persons whose valued assistance is gratefully acknowledged are two recent recipients of doctorates from Kentucky, James C. Klotter and John David Smith; and two young historians who, I trust, will soon receive their doctorates, Thomas H. Appleton, Jr., and William A. Shelton. As in the case of all my previous writings, and for so much else through many happy years, my greatest gratitude of all is offered to Suzanne Bowerfind Hamilton, my beloved wife.

H.H.

Lexington, Kentucky
October 17, 1977

Introduction

No STATE in the Union has a seal more appropriate than Kentucky's. I do not refer exclusively to Kentucky's motto—"United We Stand, Divided We Fall"—but emphasize the figures appearing on the seal. One is a gentleman in formal attire, the other a frontiersman in buckskin; and the two are shaking hands. The two figures symbolize, as no other pattern could, the two principal human (or at least male) ingredients of early Kentucky.

The frontiersman's influence of course came first. It is not hard to convince book readers or television viewers of the undoubted accomplishments and fame of Kentucky's pioneers. Daniel Boone is known the nation over. And such other frontier figures as George Rogers Clark and Simon Kenton are familiar to numerous modern Americans. Kentucky has an excellent claim to the title of the "First West." Log cabins, log houses, and log forts—known as "stations" and erected for protection from Indian assaults—reflected the norm of pioneer times. The first Kentucky frontiersmen and their families were continually aware of perils surrounding them and were every bit as inured to primitive conditions as subsequent settlers in the Far West. Boonesborough and Harrodsburg are well-remembered symbols of what living was like when Kentucky was young. But residents of many other locales, including those that became Louisville and Lexington, shared the common experiences of frontier life.

Although fundamentally western, Kentucky in its youth—and ever after—likewise was characterized by an eastern heritage identified with the Atlantic Seaboard. Originally part of Virginia, Kentucky was populated mainly by men, women, and children from Virginia, Maryland, and North Carolina.

Many of these were plain, roughhewn people with little or no exposure to assets—material or cultural—prior to crossing the mountains to their new Kentucky homes. Still, a substantial minority of those who came before 1800 had moved in beneficial social circles in the East. Such early Kentucky leaders as George Nicholas and John Breckinridge of Virginia and John Wesley Hunt of New Jersey had made the most of educational opportunities and had developed cultural standards as high as those of their eastern contemporaries. Moreover, they came west soon after the period of wilderness penetration. Thus Kentucky was quickly characterized by a prominent mix and mingle of eastern gentility and frontier earthiness.

One of the most remarkable developments was that of Lexington—the Athens of the West. Why did Lexington's population include so many residents of unusual quality? The most deterministic cause may be found in—of all things—faulty land titles. For Kentucky inherited Virginia's land "system," or lack of system, as a result of which two or more claimants to parcels of property often became enmeshed in litigation. As much of the best land lay in the Lexington vicinity or in central Kentucky's adjacent counties, the town and its environs became a happy hunting ground for lawyers from the East.

Skilled attorneys practicing in Lexington had ready access to cash income and opportunities to buy good land for themselves. They brought attractive wives with them to the Bluegrass or married lovely daughters of other "first families." They built stately mansions and, when children blessed their households, they thought not merely of elementary schooling but of secondary and even higher education. More than any other single distinction, it was Transylvania University (the "university across the woods") that gave this western "Athens" its cultural tone.

Louisville had a different sort of special reason for growing into an important community. Located at the Falls of the Ohio, it was a natural tarrying place for boatmen and passengers journeying on one of America's major rivers. As traffic and transportation burgeoned in the era of the steamboat, Louisville would shoot past Lexington in population and become Kentucky's largest city. Long before that, former field-grade officers of the Revolutionary War settled in Jefferson County on the periphery of Louisville and occupied positions of leadership. Like their counterparts in the Bluegrass and in every area where conditions for farming were especially propitious, these people—most of them Virginians—brought the institution of slavery.

Kentucky thus was a "southern" state in the sense that it was a "slave state," and also in the sense that well-to-do Virginians' architectural and other cultural tastes now were transferred west of the mountains. Yet not all Kentuckians settled on good land. Not all Kentuckians could afford mansions. Not all could afford slaves, especially settlers at the heads of hollows in eastern Kentucky. Thousands of poor whites and industrious, frugal, but by no means wealthy yeoman farmers also lived in northern Kentucky, the Green River country, and elsewhere from the winding Ohio all the way to the Tennessee line. In the 1790s, because of their numbers, there even developed a movement to eliminate slavery in Kentucky. And, while this proposal went down to defeat, the presence of numerous slaveless whites was a factor in keeping Kentucky substantially less southern than western.

The "westernness" of Kentucky was partially exemplified by the career of Henry Clay. At the turn of the century this promising Virginia lawyer settled in Lexington in his early twenties and immediately won recognition at the bar. Marrying a Kentucky heiress, he acquired land and slaves—building upon his legal reputation as a politician and going to the United States Senate before he was thirty years old. In and out of Congress time and again between 1806 and 1852, Clay almost certainly would have been prime minister if we had had the British political system.

Aspiring to the presidency on five occasions, Clay never achieved that cherished goal. Yet he was one of the three or four most prominent statesmen of his generation—a representative of western thinking and feeling, albeit with a southern exposure. The programs he advocated and the policies he endorsed were, for the most part, national in nature. And it is significant that Clay became known not as Harry of the South but as Harry of the West.

In analyzing reasons for this able man's failure to attain the pinnacle of power and prestige, one should not minimize accidents of politics—unpredictable developments that become career pivots. But one wonders whether Clay was not too much the Virginian, too much the aristocrat, too imperious to suit the preferences of his times. Andrew Jackson, not only a soldier but a lawyer and slaveholder identified with neighboring Tennessee, had—in the eyes of voters—a degree of westernness more western than Clay's own. And it may be meaningful that no Virginian or other southerner, mainly bracketed with a southern seaboard state (unless Zachary Taylor is incorrectly seen that way), was elected to the highest office after 1820 until 1964. Those southerners who won in the 1825–50 period were western-oriented southerners or, more properly, southern-oriented westerners—Jackson being the most popular.

Parts of this book deal with two presidents of the United States, one serving at the end of that same quarter century, the other coming along slightly later. Looking at their lives in outline form in biographical encyclopedias, one might suppose that Zachary Taylor and Abraham Lincoln had little in common aside from finishing first in their respective campaigns. Lincoln's profession was the law, his political experience considerable, his reading wide, his thinking deep, his chosen residence prior to the White House the capital city of a free state. A career soldier who spent forty years in the army, Taylor neither read widely nor thought deeply on most subjects, nor took any part in politics prior to his role as a presidential candidate. Taylor, moreover, was a slaveholder from young manhood until he died. A cotton planter for nearly thirty years, with plantations in Mississippi and Louisiana, he made the latter state his home when elevated to the executive mansion. How utterly different, at first glance, could the backgrounds of two men be?

Yet, in his late thirties and early forties, Lincoln enormously admired Taylor. As we shall see, the future sixteenth president worked energetically for the twelfth president's election. And when the slave-owning Taylor died, the Great Emancipator-to-be eulogized his fallen chief in a way demonstrating not only loyalty but also well-nigh incredible prescience.

For reasons that will be set forth, few students—except for experts—have appreciated this link. The striking similarity of the Taylor and Lincoln points of view on transcendent public issues of their times has been widely overlooked. In their interpretations of the federal Union, in their resolute devotion to it, and in their insistence on slavery's containment, the free-state Lincoln and the slave-state Taylor were virtually identical.

Taylor is the only president to have lived in Kentucky a great many years. The westernness of Kentucky became part of his marrow. Inheriting the slaveholding practice of older Kentuckians in and out of his family, he also inherited their Unionism. The bulk of his military service took place in the Northwest and Southwest, where Taylor's westernness was reinforced, and his Unionism with it. Both Taylor and Henry Clay (whom he defeated for the Whig nomination) were premier Unionists in 1850. These two most prominent national leaders with powerful Kentucky affiliations were adversaries who differed on methods, but they were comparably Unionistic in principle. It was Taylor—a man more direct than Clay, far humbler and less aristocratic in manner, and western in a sense that Lincoln was western—whose Unionist stand anticipated the Lincoln stand of 1861. Knowing this, we have no difficulty in viewing Lincoln as an empathetic Taylor follower.

It may be thought by some that Lincoln's birth and infancy in Kentucky had little or no effect on most of his life. True, he left Kentucky as a lad—growing to manhood in Indiana and thence heading west to Illinois. Is it, then, mere sentimentalism or antiquarianism to relate Lincoln to Kentucky? Quite the contrary. Kentucky individuals and Kentucky influences never left Lincoln no matter where he was. More consequential than what occurred to him during his seven Kentucky years was the repeated impact of Kentucky associations on the man's insight and outlook. Kentucky-type westernness accompanied Lincoln everywhere, as integral in him as it was in Taylor.

The third member of our historic trio left Kentucky when even younger than Lincoln. Yet Jefferson Davis, native of Fairview, likewise was affected by Kentucky and Kentuckians for the duration of his days. At the very age when Lincoln moved to Indiana, Davis was sent back to Kentucky from Mississippi to attend school in Washington County. There he remained a year and a half. He later spent a similar period as a college boy at Transylvania. When he was a young man his sweetheart—who became his wife in a Kentucky ceremony—was the daughter of Zachary Taylor. Like Taylor and Lincoln, Davis knew hundreds of Kentuckians from childhood and adolescence on. Davis visited Kentucky a number of times and came back to his birthplace in old age. Notwithstanding all these Kentucky relationships, the president of the Confederate States would be the leading exponent—in action—of a concept of Union diametrically different from the one in which Taylor and Lincoln believed.

A searing tragedy in Davis's life—one deeply grieving Taylor, too—will be presented in the second chapter. Though its total effect on the younger man probably never will be known, it certainly led to Davis's becoming far more of a reader and student than he had ever been before. After eight years of Mississippi isolation, when he set aside social diversions for scholarly nights and pensive days, Davis emerged intellectually reborn. Within a short time he was recognized as a foremost interpreter of Deep South, not Kentucky or nationalistic, sentiment. And the essence of his Union-secession rationale is set forth near the end of the book.

1

ABRAHAM LINCOLN
BEFORE HIS PRESIDENCY

W<small>HILE</small> Ohio, Virginia, New York, and a few other states have been closely linked to several White House occupants, most commonwealths have lacked anything more than incidental personal associations with our chief executives. In contrast, one of Kentucky's unique features is found in her intimate identification with two presidents of the United States and the sole president of the Confederacy. Abraham Lincoln and Jefferson Davis not only were born in Kentucky but had a number of Kentucky ties lasting many years. Zachary Taylor, who won the admiration of both Davis and Lincoln, grew to manhood in Kentucky and there spent over half his life. Moreover, the same pervasive issues—the federal Union's nature and future and the questions of slavery and slavery's extension—proved to be prominent in the civil careers of all three men.

On February 12, 1809, Lincoln was born in a log cabin in that portion of Hardin County which subsequently became Larue. He spent seven years in the Bluegrass state before accompanying his father, mother, and older sister to Indiana in 1816.

Although he lived much longer in Indiana and Illinois than in Kentucky, the Lincoln of adolescence and maturity was importantly influenced by people from his native state. Lincoln's parents, stepmother, wife, teachers, three law partners, and closest friend all were persons identified with Kentucky. His beau ideal of political leadership during much of Lincoln's career was the Whig champion and five-time presidential candidate, Kentucky's Henry Clay. When the Civil War came Lincoln was so conscious of Kentucky's importance to the Union that he said he hoped God would be on his side but he must have Kentucky.

The log cabin had become a widely recognized campaign symbol in 1840, two decades prior to Lincoln's first election, when William Henry Harrison ran as the first successful Whig presidential aspirant. Harrison, however, was really an aristocrat reared in a mansion near Virginia's James River and later occupying other fine houses at Vincennes in Indiana Territory and at North Bend in Ohio. Voters of 1860, on the other hand, knew there was nothing fictitious about a Kentucky cabin as Lincoln's birthplace and erstwhile home. Thus fellow partisans' presentation of Lincoln as a man of the people, who had been an infant and a child of the frontier, had a truthful ring when Honest Abe emerged as a nominee.

One facet of Lincoln's background was thoroughly misunderstood by historians and other writers until the second quarter of the twentieth century. For a long time it was widely believed that his father, Thomas Lincoln, was a Kentucky ne'er-do-well. Seeming substantiation of this "fact" came from the last of Lincoln's law partners, William H. Herndon. Some people even went so far as to assert that Lincoln's father was somebody else—making the sixteenth president illegitimate. (This idea fitted in with classical tales about the multiple gods of antiquity worshiped in Greece and Rome, who descended from the skies and impregnated earth-dwelling women. How else to account for the greatness of "the farmer's son" or "the carpenter's son"?) No fewer than fourteen prominent males, including George Washington—who died more than eight years before Lincoln was conceived—and John C. Calhoun, were brought forward as putative Lincoln sires. The whole argument, of course, was ridiculous. Still, accounts of that sort appeared in numerous books and articles. And even persons disinclined to swallow the absurdity looked down upon Thomas Lincoln as a mudsill of society.

It was not until the 1930s that re-creations of the real Thomas Lincoln came to be widely accepted. The change was due to a belated discovery that, judged by pioneer standards, Thomas had met with successes as well as failures in his Kentucky milieu. The proof appeared in the account books of Bleakley & Montgomery, proprietors of a general store in the Kentucky village of Elizabethtown. These ledgers provided evidence that, before his marriage to Nancy Hanks, Thomas Lincoln had a substantial sum of money on deposit.

On their pages are delineated, in housekeeping and clothing purchases, some of a bridegroom-to-be's preparations to become a family man. They demonstrate beyond a doubt that, in the first decade of the nineteenth century, Thomas was far from being a wastrel. Later he did have hard luck. Like Daniel Boone, he was victimized by faulty Kentucky land titles—a source of trouble for many Kentucky settlers besides the Lincolns and the Boones. In Indiana, where he attempted a fresh start, Thomas never fared so well as he had in Kentucky. He was, however, a skillful carpenter (his corner cupboards today having astronomical valuations) and he did put bread on the table. While in no sense approximating his son's intellectual or leadership abilities, Thomas minimally was a respectable person. From this paternal Kentuckian the youthful Abe undoubtedly heard much about Kentucky people, Kentucky land, and aspects of Kentucky law.

Nancy Hanks Lincoln, the president's mother, died in Indiana when her son was only nine. Like Thomas, she had long lived in Kentucky—as had Sarah Bush Johnston, the Elizabethtown widow who became Thomas's second wife. Young Lincoln and his stepmother got along well, which suggests give-and-take in their natures and also similar standards and interests. There are hints and more than hints that it was Sarah, as much as anyone else, who encouraged her stepson to read for pleasure and self-improvement and to study the grammar, mathematics, literature, and history which constituted the bases of his education. We know that he was devoted to her, just as he had been to his own mother. In early 1861 it was the Widow Lincoln he went to see on a special journey shortly before leaving Illinois to shoulder his presidential burdens.

Yet another Kentucky woman proved equally influential, and maybe more so, in a strikingly different way. Mary Ann Todd had grown up in Kentucky's principal cultural center as the daughter of a leading banker. Of excellent repute in financial circles, Robert Smith Todd was socially prominent in Lexington and a friend of Henry Clay. Young Miss Todd's family gave her advantages her future husband never had. Her formal education was far superior to his. As she was also bright and attractive, it was no surprise that—when she traveled west to visit her sisters in Illinois—she quickly became a Springfield belle.

Much controversy has clustered about the personality and character of Mary Todd Lincoln. In great measure this derives from the testimony of Herndon, who disliked Mary and was held in low esteem by her. The Mrs. Lincoln depicted by Herndon was arrogant, pompous, hopelessly neurotic, a nagger, and a spur. As Herndon would have it, she made life at the Lincolns' Springfield home so unpleasant as to cause Abraham to escape as frequently as possible—seeking relief in his law office or out on the circuit trying cases.

Enough may be learned from independent sources about the White House period when she was the first lady to indicate that Mary could indeed present problems stemming from emotionalism and extravagance. Still, on at least three counts a strong case can be made that she was far more an asset than a liability to Lincoln's career as a whole.

One of Mary's three main contributions had to do with her upbringing and family relationships. Reared amid social niceties, she was on intimate terms with the Ninian Edwardses (her brother-in-law and sister) and other influential Springfield people. She likewise maintained familial and other contacts in Lexington. Thus, to a great extent because of her, Lincoln was enabled to move in Illinois and Kentucky social circles that contrasted with the circumscribed ones of his youth.

Probably more consequential was the fact that this faithful wife and mother of four sons was intellectually capable of understanding public questions, sizing up public men, and discussing both intelligently with her husband. While evidence on this score is fragmentary, it seems that her role along such lines was more meaningful in Springfield than in Washington. (The point of their marriage at which she became most emotional and obviously neurotic followed the death of the Lincolns' most promising child, eleven-year-old Willie, during the Civil War. Nothing could be more understandable than a shattered mother's reaction to such a tragedy.)

Finally, Mary *was* a spur. Herndon, who appeared intent on denigrating her as egregiously as he did her father-in-law, could not have been more correct about her spurring. Ever ambitious, she early envisioned great things for Lincoln and no doubt aided him by goading him instead of always purveying sweetness and light. On all three counts, therefore, it must be concluded that—regardless of her flaws—Mary's relationship to Abraham's advancement tallies out as a strong plus.

If it has often been the fashion to misinterpret his wife's role, even more writers have been misled into simplistic views of Lincoln's prepresidential career. Skimming along the surface, it is easy to point out that he alone among all presidents never served in any of the following capacities—vice president, cabinet member, general, governor, senator, or longtime member of the House of Representatives. Looking at that long list, any superficial observer must find it tempting to aver that Lincoln was a political accident. How else to explain the truth that previous to 1860 he never mounted a single rung of the traditional ladder?

Approximately half the answer is available in comprehending the Illinois of Lincoln's day. It was a predominately Democratic state which never elected either a Whig governor or a Whig member of the Senate. Thus Lincoln was not the only Illinois Whig politician lacking high office in the course of his Whig years. From the Whig party's birth in the 1830s until its death throes in the 1850s, Illinois was relatively thinly populated, especially in its northern counties, and was not regarded as pivotal; hence no Illinois resident was named to any presidential cabinet. Lincoln did serve one term in the House, and so the question may be asked: "Why was he not renominated?" The answer is that, according to the custom in his district, the House nomination was passed around. Lincoln had a single shot at the office, and so did several other persons who subscribed to this gentlemen's agreement.

Looked at from a second point of view, however, Lincoln's abilities were indeed recognized—over and over—before 1860. He won election five times to the General Assembly. He was a presidential elector. He was the sole Illinois Whig in the Thirtieth Congress. In 1855 he was the Whigs' choice for United States senator; as neither he nor any other Whig could be elected, he threw his support to an Anti-Nebraska Democrat who then beat the regular Democratic candidate. In 1856 Lincoln was the runner-up for the Republican vice-presidential nomination at that party's first national convention. As a result of his spectacular 1858 canvass for the senatorship against Stephen A. Douglas, the Republican vote surpassed the Democratic vote. (Despite this, Lincoln lost to Douglas in the General Assembly because of the party lineup there.)

Then the tide turned. The northern counties of Illinois became more heavily populated, with numerous newcomers hailing from the East and opposing the extension of slavery. Many people thought the 1860 election would be decided in the newly pivotal Northwest, Illinois being a key to the outcome. Thus, nationally, it was now unquestionably an asset to be an Illinois Republican leader. According to the judgment of large numbers of Republicans, Lincoln had demonstrated eloquence and logic in the course of his joint debates with Douglas. Both geographically and ideologically, Lincoln at length was considered a remarkably "available" presidential prospect. Moreover, partly because he had never held a high political station, he did not have the handicap of old enmities which damaged rivals' claims.

The element of chance came into the picture with the Republicans' decision to do their nominating in Chicago. With the galleries full to overflowing with Illinoisans, the rafters reverberated cries of "Lincoln! Lincoln!" at the convention in the Wigwam. But let it be noted that it was Lincoln—not some other Illinois citizen—whom Republicans of the Prairie State endorsed. This enthusiasm for him resulted from the impression he had made and the reputation he had built during years of Whig-Republican frustrations. He was ready when the times were ready. Lincoln's reputation—first limited to his district, then statewide, and now extending beyond the borders of Illinois—reflected the confidence he inspired at the bar and on the stump in his policy expressions.

The melancholy side of Lincoln, not yet widely known, had no part in his 1860 image. But the humor, the whimsy, the drollery of the man had long been recognized in Illinois and now won appreciation elsewhere. When asked to prepare an autobiographical sketch, he described his education as "defective" and concluded a second statement with a pungent expression—"No other marks or brands recollected." Here was a politician without pomposity—a statesman with no suggestion of egoism. A simple man he seemed, one whose steady progress from humble beginnings to the threshold of eminence induced no semblance of conceit. Much has been written about Lincoln as the prototype of the self-made man, and this facet of his image had great appeal to voters who themselves either were or aspired to be self-made men. But here was an unusual sample of the breed—one whose self-deprecatory tone did not scale down his essential dignity—an exemplar of the American success story who continued to be humble and human.

It would be an error to say that either the personality or the character of Lincoln could not have been precisely what it was if he had had no Kentucky background. Yet it is my observation that, as late as the 1970s, certain qualities definitely including the humble and self-deprecatory are characteristic of many Kentuckians. Numerous Kentucky teachers I have known tend to downplay their knowledge, even when mastery of their subjects becomes evident in ensuing dialogue. Nor do teachers monopolize this trait; men and women in other walks of life are extremely modest in their turn. Wit and humor—so soft, so deft—often appear second nature to them. Reared by Kentuckians, associating with Kentuckians throughout his years of advancement, Lincoln was quintessentially Kentuckian in poking fun—nearly always without barbs—and in illustrating politics and so much else with extraordinary anecdotal ease.

Few Kentuckians voted for Lincoln. A state where slavery remained legal, Kentucky held fast to the compromise position which had been exemplified by Henry Clay. Neither Lincoln nor Douglas nor John C. Breckinridge, the Lexingtonian who waved aloft the banner of the Democracy's southern wing, managed to carry the commonwealth. Kentucky's 1860 electors cast their ballots for John Bell, a Tennessean who bore the standard of the Constitutional Union party. In 1864 Kentucky opposed Lincoln a second time—supporting the Democrat George B. McClellan. There was a very wide streak, predominant one may argue, of Unionism in Kentucky. Yet many Republicans' concepts of Unionism in 1860 and also 1864 were far different from the typical Kentuckian's views.

Such facts certainly should not obscure Lincoln's keen interest in the Kentucky scene in the course of his Civil War days. He kept in touch with Louisville's Joshua Speed, the old Kentucky friend of his Illinois years, and with other Kentucky Unionists. Although John C. Breckinridge cast his lot with the Confederacy as a major-general and secretary of war, his uncle, Robert J. Breckinridge, became the temporary chairman of the national convention that renominated Lincoln. And James Speed, Joshua's brother, would ultimately serve as Lincoln's attorney general.

If Lincoln at the outset lacked military experience except for a foray in the Black Hawk War, from the first he clearly comprehended Kentucky's strategic importance. In 1861 the president said that "to lose Kentucky is nearly the same as to lose the whole game." It is conceivable that Kentucky would have performed approximately as she did without a Kentucky-minded man in the White House. Nevertheless, what did occur with specific regard to Kentucky eventuated much as the prescient Lincoln had hoped and planned.

2

JEFFERSON DAVIS BEFORE HIS PRESIDENCY

IN EVALUATING the life of Jefferson Davis, one finds an almost equal number of similarities and dissimilarities with Lincoln's record. A surface evaluation, of course, points to more of the latter than the former. That part of the Davis career with which most people are familiar presents him as a Deep South Democrat, a cotton planter and slave owner, who typified secessionist sentiment and for four years headed the Confederate government. Moreover, some authors have seen Davis as a none too efficient executive who made many procedural mistakes. Almost invariably, he has been depicted as a cold person, with ice water in his veins—contrasting so totally with the warm and human Lincoln that Robert E. Lee, rather than Davis, looms as the favorite candidate for heroic stature in the Confederacy.

There have been far fewer scholarly studies of Davis than of Lincoln. Much less effort has been expended to understand the man behind the façade, and this is particularly true with respect to the antebellum decades. It is as vital to study the young Davis and the Davis of middle life as to study the Lincoln of the same developmental stages. Who was Jefferson Davis? What antecedents, youthful experiences, problems, disappointments, and successes marked or marred Davis's progress? In more than one regard the story is fascinating.

Davis's birth took place in Todd (then Christian) County, Kentucky, on June 3, 1808. The youngest of ten children, he was the son of Samuel and Jane Cook Davis, who, while not rich, were much more prosperous than Thomas and Nancy Lincoln. Though doing fairly well economically in the Bluegrass state, Samuel decided to move south before the baby was two years old. At first the family went to Saint Mary's Parish, Louisiana, and then to Wilkinson County, Mississippi, for what were hoped to be brighter financial prospects.

It was in Mississippi near Woodville that little Jeff first went to school under conditions not much better than little Abe's in Indiana. Displeased with his son's rudimentary education, Samuel decided to send him back to Kentucky for better opportunities. Leaving home when only seven years old, the boy was enrolled for a year and a half at a Roman Catholic institution—the College of St. Thomas Acquin in Washington County, Kentucky. Next came a brief period at what was called Jefferson College in Adams County, Mississippi, followed by four years at the Wilkinson County Academy near his father's home. Then, when Jeff was fourteen, he again found himself a Kentucky student, this time at Transylvania University.

Located at Lexington, Transylvania at the time was an outstanding institution of higher learning—approximate in quality to Harvard and Yale—and one of the best in the United States. Davis stayed there a year and a half (not the three years of tradition), rooming and boarding at the postmaster's house several blocks from the home of little Mary Ann Todd. He enjoyed the Lexington experience, but left in 1824 at the age of sixteen to enter the United States Military Academy. At West Point as at Transylvania, he met and mingled with many future leaders. Graduating from the academy in 1828, he became a second lieutenant in the army—all of his assignments as a subaltern being limited to the western frontier.

The picture of Davis at Transylvania and West Point is most revealing of his character and overall performance. His natural inclinations directed him toward humanities and social sciences, not mathematics or engineering. This preference no doubt explains, to an appreciable degree, his rather low standing in his class—twenty-third out of thirty-three members—at West Point, where engineering was emphasized. But that explanation is not total. What we know of his West Point record strongly suggests that he was a fun-lover, participating in scrapes, picking up demerits, and barely avoiding expulsion. Here we have a preview of the hot-blooded junior officer's later involvement in occasional escapades and personality showdowns with his superiors. Fun-loving is not the only apt adjective. Spirited, too, tells part of the story.

The most important event affecting Davis during his duty tours in the West occurred in 1832–33 at Fort Crawford in what now is Wisconsin. There, at Prairie du Chien, he fell head over heels in love with a charming girl named Sarah Knox Taylor. He was twenty-three, she eighteen, when their romance blossomed. The future president, Zachary Taylor, was the young lady's father and the post's commandant.

Member of a notable Kentucky family, "Knox"—as she was known to relatives and friends—saw nothing but good in her handsome suitor. Not so Colonel Taylor, who had at least two objections to the matrimonial hopes of Jeff and Knox. Because Mrs. Taylor had undergone multiple privations at isolated forts, the colonel sternly opposed his daughters' marrying army officers. Understandably, he wanted them to enjoy tranquility in civilization and to avoid sacrifices like their mother's. In addition, Taylor had reservations about Davis on personal grounds. One account holds that, when sitting on a court martial, Davis voted with Major Thomas Smith in opposition to Taylor. "No man who votes with Tom Smith shall marry my daughter!" the irate senior officer is said to have exclaimed. Another version contends that one evening Lieutenant Jeff had danced with an Indian maiden in a manner offensive in Taylor's eyes. Whatever the reasons for his displeasure, Zachary emphatically declared that he would not approve the Taylor-Davis match.

For the next two and a half years the young people bided their time until Knox reached her twenty-first birthday.

Meanwhile, Davis obtained a transfer to what is now Oklahoma, where the hotheadedness he had demonstrated at West Point again surfaced at Fort Gibson; and Knox left Prairie du Chien to visit kin in the Louisville area. In the spring of 1835 her fiancé resigned from the army—presumably to cancel that phase of Taylor's objections. And, although her parents still disapproved, the twenty-one-year-old Knox made her wedding plans with their full knowledge.

In various corners of the United States there are traditions that Miss Taylor eloped with Davis—from no fewer than seven communities. She did nothing of the sort. In June 1835 they became man and wife in a Jefferson County, Kentucky, ceremony attended by Knox's older sister and by many cousins in the house of her paternal aunt. Her father's older brother gave her in marriage. Mythmakers have it that she climbed out a window into the waiting arms of Davis. One wonders if it is supposed to follow that the uncle, aunt, sister, and cousins also acrobatically emerged from the window, or whether, being rational people, all those Taylors walked through doorways.

Terrible tragedy ensued. Bride and groom boarded a river packet at Louisville, the ex-lieutenant escorting the girl of his dreams to what he imagined would be an idyllic existence on a Mississippi cotton plantation. Before settling down, however, they would visit some of the Davis relatives whom Knox had never met. Thus in the late summer they were guests of Jefferson's eldest sister near Saint Francisville, Louisiana, where both newlyweds contracted malarial fever. "The country is quite healthy," Knox had assured her parents in an August letter. Alas, it was not so. The lovers had been married exactly three months when, on September 15, 1835, the bride died in the groom's arms at his sister's house in West Feliciana Parish.

Never was a widower more crushed or drained by bereavement than Jefferson Davis. He sailed to Cuba to regain his health and traveled to Washington and New York for a change of scene. But, aside from those excursions, he remained a recluse on his plantation named Brierfield for eight sorrowful years. Seeing virtually no one but his slaves and his brother

Joseph, he worked out a patriarchal system for the blacks he owned. Of immense significance is the fact that, for the first time in his life, he became an extremely diligent student. Immersing himself in books on government, history, and world literature, the once lighthearted and none-too-scholarly cadet and lieutenant reeducated himself from his twenty-seventh to his thirty-fifth year.

While attempting to assuage his grief by turning to intellectual interests, the still relatively young man benefited from the aid and devotion of an able brother. Twenty-three years Jefferson's senior, Joseph Emory Davis had become a second father to his youngest sibling after their sire Samuel's death. A veteran of the battle of New Orleans and very successful as a lawyer-planter, Joseph had a major role in Jefferson's attending West Point. Joseph, too, had a decided political orientation. And in their libraries the two men developed their mutual interests in endless discussions concerning political theory and practice. Congenial they were, and, in addition, Jefferson benefited from the generosity of Joseph. For the latter was Jefferson's financial angel.

At last, in the mid-1840s, the anchorite of Brierfield abandoned seclusion in favor of public and normal private life. Varina Howell, the beautiful Natchez brunette who became his second wife in 1845, acknowledged that the face and form of "the sainted Sarah" were never erased from his memory. Still, after the long hiatus, Jefferson was ready for a new love and a new career. A Democrat like Joseph, he lost his first political contest when he ran for the legislature in a Whig district. But when he made a race for Congress it was another story. And in late 1845, with the nineteen-year-old Varina accompanying him, he went to Washington as a member of the Mississippi delegation in the House of Representatives.

The Mexican War interrupted Davis's service on Capitol Hill. Chosen to command a regiment of Mississippi volunteers, he fought with gallantry under Zachary Taylor in the bloody battle of Monterrey. Wounded in the foot at Buena Vista, where he performed an epic exploit that helped bring victory to Taylor's troops, Davis was visited in his tent that night by his former father-in-law. I was told by Sarah Knox Davis's niece that the general then said to the colonel, "My daughter was a better judge of men than I was."

Returning home a hero to convalesce, Davis was offered a brigadier-generalship. Declining the honor, he subsequently accepted appointment to a Senate vacancy. Shortly afterwards he won election to the same seat, and in the dramatic crisis of 1850 he succeeded Calhoun as the recognized leader of the southern anticompromise forces. Davis suffered a political setback when in 1851, entering the campaign late to supplant a weaker candidate, he was narrowly defeated for Mississippi's governorship. There followed four years as head of the War Department in Washington, where he made a fine record, and then again his state sent him to the Senate, where he stayed until January 1861.

Contrasts between Davis and Lincoln in the pre-Civil War era include the southerner's far greater prominence, not only in holding offices but in distinguishing himself as an incumbent. Davis was a senator, which Lincoln was not; a cabinet officer, which Lincoln never became; and a national figure in the very period when the Illinoisan seemed a failure in politics. From Joseph, Davis obtained economic advantages—in contrast with Lincoln's unaided self-advancement. While Lincoln as a young man had been elected captain of his Black Hawk War company, this achievement paled alongside the glamour of Davis's merit in Mexico. The mantle of Calhoun appeared to fit the Mississippian better than any other resident of his region, whereas not until later did Lincoln qualify as the principal exponent of the Websterian tradition.

But if Davis's progress long went unmatched in Lincoln's career, there were similarities as well. Lincoln was defeated once, Davis twice, in popular elections. Both men had lived on the frontier and near frontier of the then Northwest. Both were identified with the Black Hawk War. Both were chosen a single time to represent their House districts in Washington. Each was a presidential elector. Each became the most respected leader in the party of his choice in the state where he made his home, a fact obscured in Lincoln's case by the circumstances previously discussed. This stature was obvious prior to the critical year of 1860, when Lincoln loomed as Illinois's premier Republican just as Davis continued to be recognized as Mississippi's outstanding Democrat.

In their personal lives dissimilarities and similarities are equally easy to recount. Born in Kentucky less than a hundred miles apart, and both leaving Kentucky as little boys, each was influenced—educationally and otherwise—by a whole host of Kentuckians. At a considerable distance from Kentucky each fell in love with, and paid court to, an appealing representative of a leading Kentucky family. Each married a Kentuckian. Each returned to Kentucky—Davis to attend the school of the Dominican friars and college at Transylvania, as well as to wed Knox Taylor; Lincoln to visit Joshua Speed at charming Farmington on the edge of Louisville, and to be a guest of Mary's father and stepmother at the Todd residence on Main Street in Lexington.

Viewed simplistically, the educations of the two men were as different as could be. The young Lincoln of backwoods Spencer County, Indiana, had a total of one year's formal schooling. And yet the adolescent Abraham, studying on his own by firelight in his father's log house, as if by a miracle managed to compensate. For, when he crossed the Wabash River at Vincennes into Illinois at the age of twenty-one, he could write well and speak well, and already he possessed leadership qualities, as within two years his peers elected him to be their company commander.

At primary and secondary as well as higher levels, from the College of St. Thomas Acquin and the Wilkinson County Academy to Transylvania and West Point, the young Davis was exposed to excellent and sustained classroom instruction which Lincoln never experienced. But what really mattered was that, as mature men, both Davis and Lincoln for years educated themselves. Lincoln, like George Washington, trained and worked as a surveyor. Then he studied law, was admitted to the bar, and became one of Illinois's most skillful attorneys—mastering the six books of Euclid along the way. With Davis's eight years of reading, studying, and thinking we have become acquainted. Rarely if ever have two opposite figures in a great national struggle devoted lengthier spans of time in their thirties and late twenties to study and serious thought.

The aggregate influence of love and marriage on the lives of both Lincoln and Davis was tremendous. In all American annals, there is no example clearer than the Davis one of a widower's intellectual growth burgeoning from the dark valley of grief. Moreover, if Davis's courtship of Knox Taylor was complicated by the intransigence of the girl's father, smooth sailing and sunny skies proved equally elusive for a time in the Todd-Lincoln romance—but for different reasons. Lincoln long was simply not sure of himself. He and his friend Speed admitted to each other that they were fearful of "nervous debility" where matrimony was concerned. On one occasion Abraham even broke his engagement to Mary. Then Speed's ultimately becoming a happy husband did much to reduce Lincoln's lingering doubts, which eventually dissolved when he and Mary wed.

The similarities between Varina Davis and Mary Lincoln were many and striking. One of the most learned and beloved men in the Natchez area was Judge George Winchester, whom Miss Howell called Great Heart. Much of her education was turned over to him by Varina's parents, who were among his admirers. At a girls' school in Philadelphia, but mainly under Winchester's direction, she made the most of opportunities to increase her information and sharpen her intellect—meanwhile becoming unusually attractive. Her schooling mirrored the same sorts of standards as Mary Ann Todd's under Lexington's Dr. John Ward and Madame Mentelle.

Like Mary, Varina unquestionably was strong willed. As early as her twentieth year, this quality manifested itself when she aggressively opposed Congressman Jeff's decision to resign his seat in the House, leave his young wife, and go off to war. Indeed, Davis failed to convince her that a West Pointer's logical station in time of war was the battlefield. Although she lost that debate when he joined the colors, her powerful will asserted itself in after times. Like Mary, Varina was deeply devoted not only to her husband personally but to enhancing his political assets. She bore six children. And when her little boy Joseph died in the executive mansion at Richmond, she suffered just as Mary suffered when Willie Lincoln was taken from her. It is a curious coincidence that each presidential household lost its brightest and most promising child while other mothers' sons were slaughtering one another in the military frightfulness of the Brothers' War.

Before her birth, Varina's family had gone to Mississippi from the northern part of the United States—her father hailing from New Jersey, where his father had served as governor. Many of Varina's kinsmen remained in the North, just as various Todd relatives and in-laws lived in the South and were identified with the Confederacy, some bearing arms against the Union. So both first ladies came to be criticized with the utmost severity and, in the main, unfairly. Faultfinders assailed Mary for sympathizing with the southern cause; and Varina, with the northern cause. Both wives were high strung, mercurial, and given to outbursts, which in no sense lightened their husbands' burdens. When the Civil War was over, both women broke down, tragic victims of nervous disorders, and both sought recovery in Europe. After a series of well-nigh incredible vicissitudes Varina's restitution was complete; Mary's, only partial.

If Lincoln's and Davis's lives had been placid, if for them true love's course had always been smooth, if their attitudes toward self-education had been different, if they had never tasted failure and all goals had been attained, one wonders whether their characters would have been as firm as history knows them to have been. No scholar ever has had access to, or ever will possess, all the materials essential to a precise answer to that question. Yet what is certain from the foregoing is that the progression of these two men, from the Kentucky of 1808 and 1809 to the 1861 presidencies of the Confederacy and the United States, was extraordinary.

Their determination to improve themselves, their triumphs over odds, and the vigor with which they did what was needed to attain distinction in a democratic society—all these reflected the tempering process at the forge of stress, sorrow, and candid self-appraisal.

3

ZACHARY TAYLOR: SOLDIER, PLANTER, PRESIDENT

IN POLITICAL ideologies, party affiliations, and partisanship itself, Abraham Lincoln and Jefferson Davis had almost wholly contrasting opinions and allegiances. One of their few points of agreement (and it was not identical in every respect) concerned Kentucky's other president—Zachary Taylor of Jefferson County.

Unlike them, Taylor was not a Kentucky native. But he lived in Kentucky for a far longer period than either of the younger men. Born in Orange County, Virginia, on November 24, 1784, little Zack was brought out west—accompanying his parents and two older brothers—to the Louisville environs when he was eight months old. He literally grew up with what became the Union's fifteenth state in 1792, seven years after his arrival. There still were Indians in Kentucky in those days. Dangerous bands of red men from across the Ohio River lurked around the log house where the youngster lived. It took time for the comparatively few white men of the area, aided by the blacks they had brought with them, to transform the wilderness into farmland and to build brick houses for their families and themselves. Lads learned to work when they were small. And, while Zack recited his letters and numbers to two schoolmasters intermittently during his boyhood, the incessant demands of farm and frontier life gave low priority to book learning.

Their primitive surroundings should not disguise the fact that, both before and after they reached the Falls of the Ohio, the Kentucky Taylors and their relations were people of ability. Back in the early colonial days their forebears had been leaders. Elder William Brewster of *Mayflower* renown was one of Zachary's direct ancestors. James Madison, who in 1787 wrote much of the American Constitution, was the Kentucky child's second cousin. And included among his future kinsmen would be Robert E. Lee and Franklin D. Roosevelt. Lieutenant Colonel Richard Taylor, young Zack's father, served creditably throughout the Revolutionary War. In the course of that struggle, he took time out to marry a Virginia girl of gentle breeding—Sarah Dabney Strother—who gave birth to her last six children in Kentucky, thus increasing her brood to a total of nine.

Nothing was more characteristic of Taylors and Taylor descendants than adherence to a military tradition. Zachary's son, grandsons, and great-grandsons were to prove themselves resourceful and valorous soldiers and sailors. One of his great-grandsons would become military governor of the Yukon, and a great-great-grandson was the longtime head of the Royal Canadian Mounted Police.

Colonel Dick's land in Jefferson County came to him as a grant in recognition of his services in the Revolution. Near him lived a number of fellow veterans, including Richard Clough Anderson (whose son Robert would defend Fort Sumter in 1861). Nearby, too, at Locust Grove resided Colonel and Mrs. William Croghan, whose son George would save Fort Stephenson in the War of 1812. And a frequent house guest of these Taylor friends was General George Rogers Clark, the famous victor of Vincennes, who was Mrs. Croghan's brother and George Croghan's uncle.

It is scarcely a surprise to learn that, reared in such an environment, Zachary and all four of his brothers who reached maturity became identified with the army for long or short periods. Zachary himself received a commission as first lieutenant of infantry in the spring of 1808 at the age of twenty-three. A captain in 1812, he successfully defended Fort Harrison on the Wabash. The first American land victory during our second conflict with Britain, this accomplishment won him the brevet of major.

The next armed encounter turned out to be less glamorous, for in 1814 at Credit Island in the Mississippi River, Major Taylor was overmatched by superior British and Indian firepower, and he retreated for the only time in his life. A third combat opportunity came in 1832 in the course of the Black Hawk campaign, when as a colonel he took part in the battle of the Bad Axe. Five years later, on Christmas Day, he commanded United States regulars and Missouri volunteers in the Florida battle of Okeechobee. For routing the Seminole and Mikasuki Indians in that fiercely fought engagement, Taylor became a brevet brigadier-general, which was his grade when the Mexican War began.

If these may be regarded as moments of drama in a long career, it should be recalled that most of Taylor's service occurred in periods of tranquility. Possibly his most signal service prior to 1846 consisted of guarding pioneer settlements and maintaining peace with Indian tribes. Except for interludes of recruiting responsibility, he never had a cushy job. Yet as often as possible he came back to Kentucky when duty and periodic leaves permitted.

In Kentucky in 1810, Taylor married Margaret Mackall Smith of Maryland. In Kentucky five of their six children were born. There he farmed in 1815–16 when, for one year, he was a civilian. There his venerable father and then his brother Hancock lived at the old Jefferson County place, where Zachary was always welcome. Taylor owned Kentucky farmland for a while. He invested in Louisville town lots and warehouses (retaining these until his death), and bought stock in two Kentucky banks.

Taylor seriously considered resigning from the army in 1821, 1838, 1841, and at other times. He did resign once, in

1815. Loving the agricultural life, he dreamed of being a full-time planter. Selling the Kentucky farm at a substantial profit, in the 1820s he bought a Deep South plantation situated partly in Wilkinson County, Mississippi, and partly in West Feliciana Parish, Louisiana. In 1841, Taylor purchased Cypress Grove plantation near Rodney, Mississippi. Unlike the moneymaking ventures preceding it, this investment proved a failure because of floods and the low price of cotton. Still he kept it so long as he lived, even when, during his presidency, he and his son Richard acquired a Louisiana sugar plantation.

As an absentee owner, Taylor entrusted the management of his planting interests and his slaves to two cousins on his mother's side of the family—first Damascus Thornton and then James Thornton. After a long period in Taylor's employ, James in the 1840s returned to Kentucky to farm on his own. Then Thomas W. Ringgold became the last of Taylor's overseers. Taylor owned 118 slaves the year of his presidential election. He bought sixty-four more a few weeks before he died. If his letters to Ringgold are to be taken as criteria, Taylor was one of the kindest of masters. When an Englishwoman and her daughter visited Cypress Grove one winter, they were shown the interior of one of the slaves' houses, which they found "extremely nice." The blacks were all "well fed, comfortably clothed, and kindly cared for." The men wore flannel trousers, their wives' dresses were made of white calico, "while almost all had woollen shawls."

Everyone was given milk to drink, a pound of meat on a daily average, as much bread as was desired, and an abundance of vegetables. Weekly every adult received coffee, butter, and flour for pastry. Taylor was especially insistent that the vegetable supply be maintained. Sheep should be butchered regularly, he directed, and made into soup for the servants' meals. He was also outspokenly opposed to exacting toil from sick field hands, advising that they be permitted to rest until they were well and strong. "Distribute . . . five hundred dollars . . . among the servants at Christmas," the manager was told one November. This should be done "in such a way as you think they deserve by their good conduct." Thus the average black received a five-dollar Christmas gift—the equivalent of forty dollars or more in 1977.

Benignity also characterized Taylor's treatment of his troops in Texas and Mexico. His tent flap was open, anyone could come to see him, and his kindnesses were proverbial. His magnanimity became evident when, at Matamoros on the Rio Grande, he ordered American doctors to give careful attention to wounded Mexicans abandoned by their superiors. Then he contributed several hundred dollars for the Mexicans' benefit. Another account depicts him aboard ship in the Gulf en route home at the war's end. Of course, the best stateroom was assigned to the general. But, turning over his quarters to wounded volunteers, he went to sleep under the sail—his bed a mattress out on the deck.

Utterly unpretentious, General Taylor rarely wore a uniform. Newcomers to his camp failed to recognize him as their commanding officer. "He looks more like an old farmer going to market with eggs to sell," declared an Indiana captain. "How little of the pronoun 'I' about him and all his acts," a youthful West Pointer from New York exclaimed. When the state of Louisiana presented Taylor with a handsome sword, with tears of gratitude he credited his victories

to the gallant officers and brave men whom he had the honor to command, and reserved to himself only a soldier's share.

What a marked exception to [other] generals on such occasions! . . . It is this noble modesty that dignifies the general, and attaches him to all his officers and men. His soldiers will ever love him, and fight with a devotion that will make up for many deficiencies in science on the battlefield.

That Taylor was deficient in military science there cannot be the slightest doubt. Unlike Davis and Lincoln, he did not use leisure opportunities in his early adult and middle years to educate or reeducate himself in anything like a proficient way. He did show sound sense at Palo Alto in the spring of 1846 by making the battle an artillery duel, as the Americans were vastly superior in that critical arm. The next day, in the hell-for-leather fray at Resaca de la Palma, he assigned cavalrymen to capture cannon—anticipating British tactics in the fatal Charge of the Light Brigade, but getting away with the risk nonetheless. At Monterrey the following September, his divided force's three-day efforts to invest the city failed. Taylor occupied it only as a result of an unauthorized armistice, which Washington superiors sharply criticized.

Owing to the Monterrey experience (which was considered a victory by most Americans), and also perhaps for political reasons, President James K. Polk lost faith in Taylor. Polk picked General Winfield Scott to land at Vera Cruz, with Mexico City Scott's objective, while Taylor was limited to a holding operation in the Monterrey vicinity. When Taylor learned that most of his seasoned fighters were being transferred to the southern column, his wrath was extreme. General Antonio López de Santa Anna got wind of what had happened and proceeded to attack Taylor's depleted contingents on the rugged terrain of Buena Vista, where the latter—again unauthorized—had advanced.

The Buena Vista battle was a nip and tuck affair contested in February 1847. Santa Anna had twenty thousand soldiers, Taylor less than one-fourth that number—fewer than five hundred of them regulars. Taylor has been criticized because temporarily he left the scene of action, beneath the shadows of the Sierra Madre, in order to check on his supportive units. But, present on the field when it really counted and conspicuously mounted on his war horse Old Whitey, he was visible to friend and foe alike—an inspiration to his men and a target for enemy shot, which penetrated his overcoat but never nicked him. Buena Vista was Taylor's most spectacular victory. More than any other single event, it propelled him to Pennsylvania Avenue.

His Mexican War triumphs notwithstanding, it is doubtful that Taylor would have reached the presidency had it not been for his personal traits. Winfield Scott, decidedly his superior as a strategist and the winner of more combat tests in Mexico, never captured the hearts of the American people. Adorned with plumes and epaulettes, tall and impressive, whereas Taylor was short and unimposing, Scott suffered under the nickname of Old Fuss and Feathers. But Old Rough and Ready had been Taylor's accolade since his service in the swamps of Florida. The simplicity, modesty, and humanity of the sixty-three-year-old border captain at first piqued many Americans' curiosity and then attracted their admiration. The more they studied the man they thought they saw, the more such scrutiny convinced them that no half-hidden flaw separated image from reality.

Just as the Mexican War was not popular everywhere in the United States, there were those—principally Democrats and northerners—who had reservations about Taylor as a political figure. The fact that he owned slaves was enough to condemn him in some northern eyes. He had never voted and never participated, even momentarily, in civil government. Hence he had no political record, and this could be construed either as liability or as asset. As a result of the war, the United States in 1848 acquired a large southwestern domain, from which the future states of California, Nevada, Utah, most of Arizona and New Mexico, and parts of Colorado and Wyoming would be carved. Should slavery be permitted to expand into some or all of this huge area? Or should slavery be contained within the fifteen states where it was legal? For a long time the public did not know how Taylor stood respecting this issue.

The uncertainty about Taylor's attitude on the principal question before the country ultimately helped, rather than hurt, his cause. The Whig party longed for a popular nominee. None of its leading statesmen ever had won the presidency. Henry Clay, now over seventy, had vainly sought the office four times and again held hopes; while some Whigs still idolized him, others identified him with defeat. Daniel Webster and fellow Whig senators also had their handicaps. Every Whig was well aware that the sole triumph of the party had come under the aegis of General William Henry Harrison, touted as the hero of Tippecanoe. The basic Whig problem was to try to transform an electoral minority into a majority. This spelled the necessity of appealing to independent voters and dissident Democrats, men who might respond with fervor to a second military nominee.

Taylor's name was first mentioned in connection with the White House in 1846. Then and the next year and fairly far into 1848, the letters he wrote in response to volunteer supporters projected rapport with those very elements—independents and Democrats disenchanted with the Polk regime. Then in April 1848 he declared himself "a Whig but not an ultra Whig." Thus, identifying himself with the party of the "outs," he concurrently held onto a substantial number of non-Whig backers. Given the problem which conditions dictated, the Taylor solution was shrewd.

Meanwhile, his backing within Whig ranks had steadily swelled in both the South and the North. The most effective part of it stemmed from Kentucky, where Taylor had influential friends, including Senator John J. Crittenden. The fact that the Crittenden Whig faction preferred Taylor to Clay in Clay's own state was a ten-strike for the general. Taylor's appeal in the Deep South naturally was strong on account of his cotton-planting, slaveholding interests. Some northern Whigs found his candidacy to their liking because they respected his army record, admired his personal characteristics, and thought he had a good chance to win. That magic word *availability* worked in his favor through the preconvention jockeying. In June 1848, when Whigs from every part of the land assembled at Philadelphia, Taylor handily won the Whig nomination by defeating Clay, Scott, and Webster.

Taylor and his running mate, New York's Millard Fillmore, opposed Democrats Lewis Cass of Michigan and William O. Butler of Carrollton, Kentucky. The nominees of both major parties avoided making definite statements on the burning issue of slavery extension. Not so a third candidate entering the contest, ex-President Martin Van Buren, who headed the Free Soil ticket. Holding their convention at Buffalo in August, the Free Soilers explicitly opposed the expansion of slavery into the soil obtained from Mexico.

Despite his personal popularity, it is possible, and perhaps probable, that Taylor would have lost the 1848 election if it had been restricted to a two-party race. The practical effect of the Van Buren entry was to split the Democratic vote in New York, which went to Taylor. Also pivotal was Pennsylvania, which Taylor carried impressively without indirect Free Soil aid. Taylor did particularly well in Kentucky, where his margin topped Clay's 1844 showing. Taylor had majorities or pluralities in exactly half the states—seven in the North, eight in the South. As in every presidential sweepstakes after 1840 until 1864, with the exception of 1852, voters as a whole did not give the victor a popular majority. His measure of triumph over Cass in the electoral college was 163 to 127.

It is illuminating to note what Davis and Lincoln said and did concerning Zachary Taylor after the general achieved military fame but before he became president-elect. As a leader of the Democrats in Mississippi, Davis adhered to the tradition of party regularity, and at the polls he supported Cass. He made no secret of the fact, however, that he was on very close personal terms with the father of his first wife. There is fragmentary evidence that pro-Taylor Whigs consulted Davis in Washington prior to the holding of the national conventions. And in the postconvention campaign Davis maintained the lowest of partisan profiles.

Earlier the Democratic senator from Mississippi had done much to impress the public with his high opinion of Old Rough and Ready. In 1847, Davis wrote that—brilliant as were Taylor's victories in the war—"those who . . . know . . . him best will equally . . . honor him for the purity, the generosity, and . . . magnanimity of his private character. His colossal greatness is presented in the garb of the strictest republican simplicity." In 1848, Davis added that Taylor's life —"wholly devoted to his country"—had become "a pyramid," beautiful in simplicity, sublime in grandeur. Taylor's obelisk, said Davis, should resemble the Bunker Hill Monument— "its head amid the clouds," despising "assaults of . . . creeping things that crawl around its base." No eulogy of Taylor after his death would surpass this tribute.

While Lincoln then said nothing of comparable eloquence, he intimately identified himself with the Taylor candidacy both before and after the Whig convention. Throughout the campaign year, he was a northwestern rarity within an active congressional group ardently supporting the general. Following the Philadelphia nomination, Lincoln toiled for Taylor, franking hundreds of documents and delivering a pungent anti-Cass speech on Capitol Hill. Then he campaigned briefly in Maryland and Delaware and extensively in Massachusetts and Illinois. As would be expected of one who was both an original Taylorite and a dedicated Whig, Lincoln cast his ballot at Springfield for Taylor and carried his enthusiasm over into the postinauguration months.

As chief executive, Taylor took a strong Unionist position in the northern Whig meaning of the word *Unionist*. Sternly opposing the compromise ideas of Senators Clay and Douglas, he offered a "President's Plan," according to which California and New Mexico would enter the Union as states. Taylor could have let the matter go at that, without contributing direct or indirect White House action or influence. Instead, he did everything in his power to make sure that the people of California and New Mexico would present free-state constitutions when applying to Congress for admission.

Manifestly, this position was anathema to most southern Democrats and Whigs alike—and a happy surprise for numerous northerners. Not a few politicians on both sides of the Mason-Dixon Line were astonished that a man of southern residence and associations, a planter and a slaveholder, would do as Taylor did. Had they known that the planter was in the process of buying another plantation, or that the slave owner would soon acquire more slaves, their amazement would have been compounded in learning details of his activities respecting California and New Mexico.

The Whig in the White House developed the President's Plan even though the Democrats had a majority in the Senate and a plurality in the House of Representatives. Every northern Whig senator, with two exceptions, supported the Taylor proposal. So did many northern Whig representatives and a scattering of other congressmen. There is every indication that the Compromise of 1850 could never have passed if

29

Taylor had lived. Even after his death, it failed to pass with the Clay stipulations and in the Clay form despite Millard Fillmore's throwing the weight of presidential prestige and patronage power on the side of the Clay adherents. Taylor was president fewer than 500 days. In that brief period, however, he had a powerful impact on political developments.

The discovery of gold in California, accounts of the treks to El Dorado, and reports from the Sacramento Valley itself have concentrated much historical attention on 1848 and 1849. The year 1850, however, was replete with drama of its own, and not a few episodes in and out of Washington naturally involved President Taylor.

The state of Texas claimed what is now the Santa Fe region of New Mexico. Units of the United States Army were stationed there under an officer who served as the area's military governor. There was a very real danger of a Santa Fe confrontation between Texas militiamen and the United States troops. (Texas being a slave state, possession of the disputed domain was a factor in slavery's extension or containment.) Taylor made no secret of his resolution to uphold the national authority if Texas chose to challenge it. Not long before he died on July 9, 1850, it was understood in Washington that he planned to strengthen the Santa Fe garrison and that, if civil war erupted as a result of a southwestern clash, he would personally take the field against any and all disunionists.

Such determination on the president's part came as no surprise to observers familiar with the Washington scene. Taylor's Inaugural Address on March 5, 1849 had been a rather negative one. But in his State of the Union Message the following December, he declared that the Union's dissolution "would be the greatest of calamities. . . . Upon its preservation must depend our own happiness and that of countless generations to come. Whatever dangers may threaten it, I shall stand by it and maintain it in its integrity to the full extent of the obligations imposed and the powers conferred upon me by the Constitution."

In February 1850 at Fredericksburg, Virginia, the president reemphasized his stand: "As to the Constitution and the Union, I have taken an oath to support the one and I cannot do so without preserving the other, unless I commit perjury, which I certainly don't intend to do. We must cherish the Constitution to the last. There . . . will be local questions to disturb our peace; but, after all, we must fall back upon" George Washington's farewell advice and "preserve the Union at all hazards."

Thus the New Mexico part of the crisis should not be viewed as an isolated episode. In the same month that Taylor spoke in Virginia, the capital seethed with threats of secession and disruption. That winter a North Carolina Whig congressman (who would become a Confederate general) described the south as ready for disunion. "The breach is widening," a Minnesotan feared. The "apprehension . . . that a separation of the Union would take place . . . is now universal."

A Kentuckian close to Taylor wrote to Crittenden (now Kentucky's governor) that two senators from the South "produced quite a panic . . . by declaring that, unless something was very soon done, events . . . would render a dissolution of the Union certain." Edward Everett of Massachusetts said: "There never was a period when the continuance of the Union seemed to me so precarious." There were fistfights with congressmen as combatants and at least one threatened duel. Many representatives of the people carried pistols on Capitol Hill. In April Mississippi's senior senator (not Davis) pointed a loaded weapon at Missouri's senior senator on the floor of the historic chamber, while the putative target bared his chest and cried: "Let the assassin fire!"

To an appreciable degree, 1850 provided a preview of 1861 with respect to presidential attitudes, just as the nullification winter of 1832–33 had anticipated 1850. There were differences between nullification and secession, and indeed Jefferson Davis came to consider them as "antagonistic principles." Nevertheless, Andrew Jackson's stand on the South Carolina question nearly eighteen years before bore an unmistakable resemblance to Zachary Taylor's in connection with Texas and New Mexico. Like Taylor, Jackson was a slaveholder and a southerner. But both also were westerners with tremendous devotion to the nation as a whole. The nonslave-holding Abraham Lincoln was imbued with Unionist convictions like theirs and, as president, would behave much as they had. Thus Taylor, in an important sense, was a Jackson-Lincoln link.

It was a measure of President Taylor's warm personal regard for Davis that the senator and Varina were treated as members of the family. In Taylor's time they were in the White House as constantly as if they had been blood kin. This was true despite the fact that Davis diametrically opposed Taylor's interpretation of the Union and extension issues. "I wish you to pursue that course," the chief executive wrote Davis (then in Mississippi) in September 1849, ". . . which your good sense, interest" and "honor . . . prompt you to do. . . . The family . . . join me in kindest regards to your better self, your worthy brother & his most excellent lady as well as yourself. . . . Wishing you all continued health and prosperity [,] I remain truly Your Friend Z. TAYLOR."

Albert J. Beveridge was partly responsible for misconceptions of Taylor's treatment of Abraham Lincoln. In his Lincoln biography Beveridge wrote that the only appointive post offered the Illinois Whig by the Taylor administration was the secretaryship of Oregon Territory. Yet at first he had the refusal of the General Land Office commissionership, a prestigious office just below cabinet level. Taylor also offered him the Oregon governorship, which Lincoln declined. These were as good positions as went to anyone living west of the Ohio-Indiana line. Instead of being rated "a failure" (as Beveridge asserted), Lincoln received substantial recognition from the Whig president he helped nominate and elect.

Lincoln, moreover, delivered as sensitive and accurate an estimate of Taylor's presidential significance as any contemporary. In his Chicago City Hall eulogy of July 25, 1850, the lawyer from Springfield said that the presidency "is no bed of roses." Taylor, like others, "found thorns within it." Still Lincoln believed that, "when General Taylor's official conduct shall come to be viewed in the calm light of history," he will be found to deserve as little censure "as any who have succeeded him."

Not "all" patriotism and wisdom had died with Taylor, the ex-congressman declared, but "wisdom and patriotism . . . are wholly inefficient and worthless, unless they are sustained by the confidence and devotion of the people." In Taylor's death, "we have lost a degree of that confidence. . . . I fear the one great question of the day is not now so likely to be acquiesced in by the different sections of the Union, as it would have been, could General Taylor have been spared to us."

4

PRESIDENT LINCOLN

ONE OF THE persons soon to succeed Taylor turned out to be Lincoln himself. After four years of relative political quiescence, Taylor's eulogist was brought back to the alarums and excursions of public life by the enactment of the Kansas-Nebraska Bill. From 1854 he marched—seemingly through a series of defeats, but in reality from strength to greater strength. The most colorful of Lincoln's multiple activities of the 1850s were his joint debates with the "Little Giant" Douglas. After their conclusion in the autumn of 1858, he loomed ever larger as a national figure, a development which his Cooper Union speech in early 1860 enhanced. The overriding issue in both those years was the same as in Taylor's time. It continued to be compounded of two parts: the extension or containment of slavery and the nature and future of the Union.

There has been speculation that, had the Democratic party remained united, neither Lincoln nor any other Republican could have won the 1860 election. Such a possibility vanishes when state-by-state statistics are examined. Lincoln carried virtually the entire North by clear state majorities, third and fourth parties having no role like the Free Soilers' in New York twelve years before. It must be remembered that the Republicans of 1860 did not campaign in favor of slavery's abolition.

Nor did they advocate civil war. With the exclusion of slavery from the West as their rallying cry, their posture in this regard was identical with Zachary Taylor's a decade earlier.

Yet much had happened during that decade to heat northerners' and southerners' blood. The Fugitive Slave Law, the agitation over Kansas, the caning of Charles Sumner, the Dred Scot decision, and the hanging of John Brown widened fissures of misunderstanding into chasms too broad to bridge. Presidents Millard Fillmore, Franklin Pierce, and James Buchanan—northerners all—became intensely unpopular in the region whence each had come. Southerners detested the Republican party, which they correctly considered sectional and which they feared would trample on states' rights and do away with slavery everywhere.

There were many statements in 1860 by politicians and others in the South that, if a Republican should be chosen for the presidency, southern secession would result. In December, a month and a half after Lincoln garnered the essential electors, South Carolina with a flourish led the way out of the Union. Mississippi, Florida, Alabama, Georgia, and Louisiana followed in January 1861. Texas on February 1 brought the total to seven. The provisional government of the Confederate States of America came into being at Montgomery, Alabama, with Jefferson Davis in the presidential chair. All these developments occurred before Lincoln, on March 4, supplanted Buchanan in Washington.

Some of Lincoln's fellow Republicans (Charles Francis Adams of Massachusetts, for example) had serious reservations about him at the outset. Lacking executive experience and still a stranger to many easterners, he confronted a graver crisis than had any of his predecessors. William H. Seward of New York, whom Lincoln named to head the Department of State, was so dubious of his chief's abilities that within a month he proposed that he—not Lincoln—should make major policy decisions. In due course the president demonstrated that, while he had great respect for Seward, he had not the slightest intention to abdicate authority.

Prior to March 4, at Lincoln's request, Seward had drafted a proposed final paragraph for the Inaugural Address:

I close. We are not we must not be aliens or enemies but fellow countrymen and brethren. Although passion has strained our bonds of affection too hardly they must not, I am sure they will not be broken. The mystic chords which proceeding from so many battle fields and so many patriot graves pass through all the hearts and all the hearths in this broad continent of ours will yet again harmonize in their ancient music when breathed upon by the guardian angel of the nation.

Lincoln altered Seward's version as follows:

I am loth to close. We are not enemies, but friends. We must not be enemies. Though passion may have strained, it must not break our bonds of affection. The mystic chords of memory, stre[t]ching from every battlefield, and patriot grave, to every living heart and hearth-stone, all over this broad land, will yet swell the chorus of the Union, when again touched, as surely they will be; by the better angels of our nature.

Just compare the two passages. Read them again. Read them aloud. As Carl Sandburg understood and stated so lucidly, Lincoln not only shortened what Seward had proposed but "transmuted it into slightly different meaning and a distinctly changed verbal music." Putting the matter more bluntly, Lincoln produced a beautiful jewel while Seward's product was flawed. Most persons approaching Lincoln's genius for expression have not begun to match him in action as well, and the reverse is equally true. The sixteenth president was both natural leader and word artist. Eventually, in world opinion, he would surpass Seward and every other American politician of his era in the significance of both what he did and what he said.

From the hour that Confederate cannoneers fired on Fort Sumter in April 1861, Lincoln bent every effort to mobilize and shape the forces of the Union. Although four additional southern states joined the Confederacy in April and May, the

36

Abraham Lincoln as a lawyer in Springfield, Illinois, 1858
Courtesy of University Libraries, The University of Nebraska-Lincoln

Lincoln as president in 1865
Courtesy of Louis A. Warren Lincoln Library and Museum
Fort Wayne, Indiana

The Capitol during Lincoln's first inauguration, March 4, 1861
From *Frank Leslie's Illustrated Newspaper*

Zachary Taylor, an unfinished engraving on an 1848
daguerreotype. His Baton Rouge home is in the background.
Courtesy of the author

Zachary Taylor, a daguerreotype of the 1846-1850 period
Courtesy of Chicago Historical Society

Jefferson Davis as secretary of war (1853-1857)
Courtesy of Chicago Historical Society

Jefferson Davis as president of the Confederacy
Courtesy of the Mississippi Department of Archives and History

The inauguration of Jefferson Davis as president of the
Confederacy in Montgomery, Alabama, on February 18, 1861.
From *In Memoriam Jefferson Davis* (Charleston, S.C.:
Walker, Evans & Cogswell Co., 1890)

four slave commonwealths of Delaware, Kentucky, Maryland, and Missouri did not. Kentucky tried to be neutral, which was one reason the president gave the state of his birth so much of his attention.

As the Civil War proceeded, there was fighting in Kentucky as well as in Missouri and Maryland—and of course much combat in Virginia and farther south. Especially in the borderland, brother bore arms against brother, and father against son. Kentucky families like the Taylors, Clays, Crittendens, and Breckinridges split down the middle. Still Lincoln's 1861–62 attempts to prevent the number of Confederate states from increasing succeeded. And despite Lincoln's having polled only 1,365 Kentucky votes, far more Kentuckians saw fit to join the northern than the southern army.

In the East there was much to hearten the South in the initial eighteen months of the struggle. The first battle of Bull Run (mid-1861) can only be described as a northern disaster or a southern success. Simon Cameron did a poor job as head of the War Department. George B. McClellan, the young officer then entrusted with weightier responsibilities than any other Union general, performed ably as a trainer of troops but (in Lincoln's words) suffered from "the slows" as a field commander. In the spring of 1861 the Confederates moved their capital from Montgomery to Richmond. There were hopes in the North that, in an elaborate 1862 campaign, McClellan could not only score spectacular victories on the peninsula between the James and York rivers but attack Richmond as well. Ten weeks of hard fighting ensued in that storied Peninsular Campaign. But the southern will to fight, southern leadership, and southern troop dispositions dashed the expectations of Lincoln and compelled McClellan's men to return north—their objectives unattained.

Lincoln's good judgment in supplanting Cameron with Edwin M. Stanton went unmatched by his experiments with a series of none too competent generals in the East. While Union soldiers did not lose all their battles there, they lost more than would have been the case under better direction. In the western theater of operations, northern fortunes fared far more favorably. There a part of the North's advance derived from the insight and gumption of Ulysses S. Grant, who captured two key Tennessee forts and achieved other successes. In April 1862, at Shiloh in west Tennessee, Confederates under Albert Sidney Johnston had Union regiments on the run until Johnston was mortally wounded and the southerners consequently lost their momentum. On the second bloody day at Shiloh, a reinforced Grant reversed the tide of battle. The South's invasion of Kentucky in the summer and early fall of 1862 ended in Confederate retreat from the state after the battle of Perryville.

More inspiring to the North than these events, however, was the occupation of New Orleans in April 1862 by David Glasgow Farragut. Leading naval units up the Mississippi River from the Gulf of Mexico, this grizzled sea dog was responsible for an accomplishment more striking than anything previously done by Union troops on land. Like Farragut and Grant, Lincoln clearly saw the Mississippi's tremendous significance to the war in the West. Thus, strategically, the fact most favorable to the Union cause as a whole was the North's control by summer's end of the entire river except for a 250-mile stretch between Vicksburg and Port Hudson.

The president composed the Emancipation Proclamation in the same period and then made it official on January 1, 1863. Like a number of Lincoln's decisions, it was bound to be controversial—and nowhere more than in Kentucky. "Kentucky joined the Confederacy when the Civil War was over" is an oft heard expression today. Yet Kentucky's increased empathy with the seceded states really began when emancipation was bruited.

Lincoln at the time was more deeply concerned about England and France than Lexington and Louisville. He wanted to do all in his power to preserve British and French neutrality, and he believed that endorsement of a moral issue would impress people and governments abroad. He also regarded the proclamation as having a practical military value, because the only blacks emancipated by the document's provisions were those residing in areas controlled by the Confed-

38

eracy. As the northern forces pushed ahead, more and more of the slaves would be freed, and it was thought that the prospect of freedom would encourage slaves to become a disruptive element behind enemy lines. Why should hundreds and thousands of Kentuckians become so upset by something not immediately affecting them? Because they considered the proclamation a "foot in the door" for emancipation everywhere.

The year 1863 was significant in other ways. On July 4, John C. Pemberton capitulated at Vicksburg to General Grant. As a result of this and related developments, Lincoln soon was warranted in exclaiming: "The Father of Waters again goes unvexed to the sea." The evening of the same Fourth of July, amid a torrential storm, Robert E. Lee headed toward the Potomac after three days of fighting at Gettysburg. The denouement of the Confederacy's Pennsylvania campaign, this was another major Union victory, even though George G. Meade's men were unable to pursue and capture the retreating southerners.

The business of killing continued for nearly two more years. While some of the most ferocious slaughter occurred in Tennessee and Georgia, by mid-1864 attention was mainly concentrated on the struggle in Virginia. With every imaginable material advantage and consistently outnumbering his ill-equipped foe, Grant (long since transferred from the West) doggedly drove Lee back until on April 9, 1865, Marse Robert surrendered at Appomattox. Meanwhile, the preceding November, Lincoln had won reelection by 212-21 over the Democrat McClellan. His second inauguration took place on March 4, 1865. Lincoln lived until April 15, when he died from a bullet wound inflicted by John Wilkes Booth at Ford's Theater the night before.

By that time the Civil War was all but over, with Joseph E. Johnston surrendering on April 26 and other Confederate commanders following the Lee-Johnston example. Deaths of southern uniformed personnel during the four-year struggle totaled 164,981; northern fatalities were 359,528. Of these, 74,524 and 110,070 respectively were battlefield casualties. Many northerners and southerners suffered serious or minor wounds, with some of the wounded to be handicapped forever.

The monetary cost of the war to the Union is estimated at $4,486,198,881—approximately four and a half billions. Pensions and other veteran-related expenditures by the United States government in after years involved huge additional outlays. The financial burdens of the South were so heavy that they cannot even be estimated. After the surrender Confederate money and bonds were worthless. And the economic plight of ruined individual southerners had no counterpart in northern states.

The Civil War achieved Lincoln's principal purpose, the preservation of the Union. Due partly to the Emancipation Proclamation and partly to the Thirteenth Amendment (ratified in December 1865), chattel slavery was abolished. Northern industry and commerce, impressive prior to the conflict, boomed increasingly during and after it. The Civil War ushered in an era when rail transportation and then steel vastly expanded industrial growth. On numerous counts the war constituted the most important event of the nineteenth century in the Western Hemisphere.

From 1865 to 1900, and throughout the twentieth century to date, the name of Abraham Lincoln has been honored as the grand symbol of Union and freedom. As commander-in-chief of approximately 2.25 million fellow Americans (most of them civilians in uniform), he was held in respect by legions of survivors for the duration of their lives. The Grand Army of the Republic, a Union veterans' organization popular and powerful for decades, had Lincoln as its principal hero. The Republican party, not just every four years at its national conventions but month in and month out utilizing the written and spoken word, extolled the man who had borne its standard in its first and second electoral triumphs. Books, articles, and reproductions of oil paintings and photographs were extensively circulated, bringing the Lincoln story and the Lincoln likeness into millions of American homes. School children memorized the Gettysburg Address, and in the pulpit and on the platform familiar passages from other Lincoln speeches were extensively quoted and taken as texts. Moreover, not mere popularity or respect but even reverence came to characterize the way in which untold numbers of people regarded Lincoln as the epitome of virtue. In many hearts and minds he became sanctified.

The real-life Lincoln had wit and humor and could be earth-earthy in the yarns he spun. The live Lincoln could temporize and compromise when, in his best judgment, a situation called for such expedients. The dead Lincoln, on the other hand, often was "restored" in the mind's eye as a sort of lay saint—an idealist who invariably took the high road—ever right and never wrong. There was a tendency to lose sight of the flesh-and-blood Lincoln in the fervor of idolatry. Biographers devoted to the truth had a wonderful tale to tell, but they long experienced difficulties in re-creating the mortal man with all the competition of the mythmakers.

In the course of his quadrennium in the White House, Lincoln—like presidents preceding and following him—had his full share of critics. He was caricatured as a gorilla, an ape, a tyrant, a dictator, a buffoon.

While it was to be expected that many southerners would dislike or even loathe the head of the adversary government, men and women of embattled Dixie had no monopoly on the anti-Lincoln harshness and hate. In the North even members of his own party assailed him out loud or insidiously in whispers. Radical Republicans like Thaddeus Stevens were themselves convinced, and sought to persuade others, that the president was too moderate and too weak. Then, too, there were war-weary northern Democrats and Republicans who saw him as a bloodstained butcher thrusting young men interminably into the maw of war, meanwhile chuckling at cabinet sessions that "this reminds me of a little joke." History records a period of strong opposition to Lincoln's second election, and a time when he himself thought he would lose. His most dangerous opponents, in the political context, were neither southerners nor Democrats but Republicans, prominently including some of Lincoln's own appointees.

The Lincoln of 1861–65, like the Lincoln of the backwoods

41

and the prairies and the boy Lincoln of Kentucky, is a credible Lincoln who merits far greater esteem than the icon of the deifiers. His manner was humble, his humility genuine; yet his genuineness did not eliminate either exemplary political courage or a second quality of astute public men—the ability to delay and watch and wait for the best opportunities to act resolutely.

It is conceivable that the Union cause would have emerged victorious, and that the slaves would have been freed, without Lincoln in the presidency. But what we know—without a shadow of doubtfulness obtruding—is that these events did occur with the erstwhile one-term Whig congressman in charge. Today most Americans count their nation fortunate not only because unity was reattained and slavery abolished, but also because the crisis gave Lincoln's contemporaries and posterity such a remarkable exemplar.

5

PRESIDENT DAVIS

THE JEFFERSON DAVIS who took the oath as president of the Confederate States of America, under the provisional arrangements of February 1861, would have preferred another role. Before his election at Montgomery, Mississippi had named him the major-general in command of her troops. With his West Point training and Mexican War background, his attraction to this assignment is not surprising. Still, the South possessed a larger supply of military than executive talent. One of Davis's undeniable career assets was his four-year record as Secretary of War under Franklin Pierce. In the United States Senate, too, he had gained a widespread reputation in both South and North as a premier spokesman for his section; had headed the Senate Military Affairs Committee; and had become well acquainted with both northern and southern leaders.

In view of the northern stereotype of Davis during and after the Civil War as a traitor or southern archfiend, it is pertinent to recall the respect in which he was held by many northerners in antebellum times. Visiting New England for his health in the summer of 1858, he had been invited to speak at Portland, Maine, where he emphasized the "national sentiment and fraternity which made us, and . . . alone can keep us, one people." That year Bowdoin College made him an honorary doctor of laws.

Later in 1858, at a Democratic ratification meeting in Boston's Faneuil Hall, the senator from Mississippi said: "If I were selecting a place where the . . . extreme asserter of democratic state rights doctrine should go for his text, I would send him into the collections of your [Massachusetts] historical association. . . . The great stone your fathers hewed . . . [was] the fit foundation for a monument to state rights!" Davis's Faneuil Hall remarks were applauded or cheered forty-seven times. Among those favorably impressed by him on that occasion was Benjamin F. Butler, the future Beast Butler or Spoons Butler of New Orleans notoriety, who at the 1860 Democratic National Convention in Charleston would back Davis for president of the United States on fifty-seven ballots.

It must not be imagined that Davis talked one way in Maine and Massachusetts and New York (where he also drew resounding cheers in 1858) and a different way in Mississippi or the District of Columbia. Consistently he defended the institution and the constitutionality of slavery. Invariably his major theme was the states' rights principle. Repeatedly he made it clear that he did not favor secession except as a last resort. And more than once he declared that he would approve a North-South accommodation, provided fundamentals were not abandoned, in lieu of plunging the American people into a military bloodbath.

Nor was Davis considered anything like one of the most extreme of southerners in the South itself. He was no firebrand of the type of South Carolina's Robert Barnwell Rhett, Alabama's William L. Yancey, or Texas's Louis T. Wigfall. In 1861 no member of the latter group stood a chance for the Confederacy's presidential post. Both Robert Toombs and Howell Cobb of Georgia, and several others, had supporters who preferred them for the office. Indeed, remote on his plantation, Davis thought arrangements had been made for Cobb to be selected. But in the minds of many influential men who gathered that winter at Montgomery, Davis seemed the person who—both ideologically and administratively—was best qualified to perform the presidential duties.

The problems confronting Davis would have dismayed anyone deficient in the courage and determination he possessed. The total population of the eleven Confederate states added up to approximately 9 million (including 3.5 million slaves), compared with nearly 19 million in the nineteen free states and 3.1 million in the four slave states which did not break with the Union. The South had only one-quarter of the country's wealth, one-eighth of the manufacturing, and less than one-third of the 30,000 miles of railway track. In shipping, as in banking and industrial productivity, the South was at a similar disadvantage. And so the story went in numerous material categories, having a direct bearing on the conduct and the outcome of a colossal struggle.

Another big handicap for the Confederacy was that it was a new nation. It had no governmental structure created over a period of years. Brick by brick, and inch by inch, it had to be built from the foundation up. Worst of all, as matters evolved, it was essential to accomplish so trying a task while concurrently waging a war.

At the outset Davis seems to have expected a long, hard war. But, like Lincoln and his advisers, Davis and other southern leaders hoped the conflict would be short. Like so many southerners, they placed great confidence in southern generals and (most of all) in the South's military tradition. For roughly one year the Confederacy did hold advantages in those respects. Initially, there was a certain amount of evidence bolstering the hope that northerners were unwilling to make substantial sacrifices for the Union cause. Many southern people saw the North as a region which put priorities on manufacturing and shopkeeping, with its men intent on making money and deficient in the martial spirit.

In late 1860 and early 1861 such respected northern spokesmen as Horace Greeley of the *New York Tribune* offered the opinion that southern states should be permitted to "go in peace" if it was their judgment that they could do better outside the Union than in it. "Whenever a considerable section of our Union shall deliberately resolve to go out," Greeley asserted, "we shall resist all coercive measures designed to keep it in." Even Winfield Scott, the aged general at the head of the United States Army when Lincoln and Davis came into power, had thoughts and feelings akin to the journalist's.

"All we ask is to be let alone," Davis told the Confederate Congress on April 29, and "that those who never held power over us shall not now attempt our subjugation by arms." Yet the depart-in-peace solution or quasi-solution quickly gave way to sterner views above the Mason-Dixon Line after the firing on Fort Sumter. Assuredly the North would not, and did not, let the South alone. Both Lincoln and Davis called up troops—the former 75,000 and the latter 100,000. Combat and preparation for combat permeated northern policy and programs after the first battle of Bull Run. And so the Confederacy, with all the disadvantages mentioned here and others comparably deterministic, came face to face with the reality that a long war stretched ahead.

Ah, but did not the South possess one impressive economic asset in the midst of all the evident liabilities? "Cotton is king!" the most optimistic of the southerners proclaimed. Were not the cotton mills of Massachusetts dependent on the staple from southern fields? Would not the inaccessibility of the raw material hamstring New England's manufacturing of finished products, deprive northerners of essential textiles, and play hob with the North's economy as a whole? It was arguable, too, that Britain, France, and other European countries would go on needing American cotton and buying it in large quantities as in the past.

Even with southern coasts blockaded by the United States Navy, could not the Confederacy rely upon—and profit from—a flourishing British and French trade by running the blockade and resorting to other expedients? Britain and France, furthermore, might have something to say on the subject of northern attempts to interfere with international trade, perhaps even siding with the southern cause diplomatically and militarily.

Thus roseate expectations of wishful thinkers had a place in the Confederacy alongside pessimists' gloom, just when southern field performance, chiefly in Virginia, brought a tingle of pride and a glow of confidence to southern soldiers and noncombatants alike. Somehow green recruits were uniformed, trained, and battle-hardened. Somehow the Tredegar Iron Works at Richmond and other establishments performed miracles of arms production. Somehow Confederate vessels, adopting hit-and-run tactics, assaulted and damaged and burned northern shipping. Confederate heroes—how knight-like they seemed, and how inspirational to the men they led. Robert E. Lee and Albert Sidney Johnston in particular resembled cavaliers of old, champions in shining armor, devotees to the cause.

Unlike Lincoln, Davis had long enjoyed acquaintance with scores of the most resourceful officers in America. Many southern generals were his warm personal friends. Not a few he had known as a West Point cadet. The president of the Confederacy had faith in the abilities of commanders whose development he had professionally observed. He frequently stood by them even when critics grew impatient with them or found fault with their performances. Witness the case of Albert Sidney Johnston when, after Fort Donelson's fall, the Tennessee General Assembly dispatched a delegation to Davis requesting the removal of Johnston "because he is no general." If Johnston "is not a general," the president replied, "we had better give up the war, for we have no general."

One of the complaints lodged against Davis, by contemporaries and by scholars, concerned this very trait of loyalty to subordinates. In Johnston's case such criticism on the part of historians has not been pervasive for the simple reason that Johnston at Shiloh—to the moment of his tragic death—acquitted himself magnificently. The president, however, also saw virtues in Braxton Bragg which other people failed to discern, and he was criticized for giving Bragg assignments which more logically might have been bestowed elsewhere. The case of Lucius B. Northrop has been widely considered another example of misplaced confidence.

Secondly, Davis's relations with Joseph E. Johnston and P. G. T. Beauregard have long been debated in scholarly circles. As the war went on, it became evident that both these generals hated the president. There were times when each of them

47

functioned or failed to function in ways which, in Davis's view, harmed the war effort. But, as each had a very vocal clique in the Confederate Congress, there were important occasions when Davis entrusted them with heavy responsibilities despite grave personal reservations. Indeed, it may be said that Davis erred more seriously in turning the other cheek to his enemies than in lending support to his friends.

A third kind of criticism stemmed from Davis's real or alleged interference with procedures in the field. One point of attack has to do with the supplanting of Joseph Johnston with John Bell Hood after the former fell back in Georgia as the forces of William T. Sherman advanced. Here the accusation is that Hood wasted the opportunities for an effective counterattack husbanded by his predecessor. Yet Davis's admirers underscore his record in connection with Robert E. Lee, stating that it reflects creditably on the president's readiness to delegate when a general was worthy of delegation. Here we are discussing a degree of confidence such as Davis had earlier reposed in the command capacity of Sidney Johnston. Clearly, Lee respected Davis just as Davis respected Lee. The latter received tremendous military and moral encouragement from his fellow West Pointer in the Confederate executive mansion.

A fourth allegation, popular with some writers concentrating on the war in the West, is that many southern units ought to have been transferred from Virginia to Tennessee. The contention has been that the Army of Tennessee remained undermanned at a juncture when Lee could have spared a portion of his troops. Such reinforcements, so the story goes, would have increased the problems of Sherman and of Grant (before he came east) giving the Confederacy a better opportunity to score Tennessee or Georgia victories in lieu of the defeats that eventuated. Was Lee a victim of military myopia, limiting his vision to the needs of his own native Virginia? Was Davis guilty of a major executive error in permitting Lee's judgment to prevail? Those questions are answered affirmatively by this segment of the critics.

Davis's vulnerability to critical fire in his role as commander-in-chief was and is greatest in regard to strategy. It has

been stated that the president, and therefore the Confederacy, was too defense-minded at the start of the fighting and
remained too defense-minded throughout. The accusation is
made despite Lee's Maryland thrust in 1862 and his Pennsylvania incursion the next year—efforts halted by Union successes at Antietam and Gettysburg. Both during and after the
war, particularly telling charges have been directed against
Davis's record respecting Vicksburg. A strong case may be
made that there was a stage, during Grant's preparations to
besiege the Mississippi city, when most of John C. Pemberton's command could have been withdrawn to fight elsewhere
another day. Also it has been repeatedly argued that, unlike
Lincoln, Davis failed to comprehend the enormous importance of controlling the Mississippi River. Here, it is emphasized, the military amateur in the Washington White
House proved infinitely more prescient than the West Point
alumnus.

In studying Davis in the military overview, several significant positive features should be identified. Despite formid-
able opposition, he insisted on the formation of a national
army controlled by national—not state—authority. He proved
practical, too, in resorting to conscription. He used slaves as
auxiliaries and, finally, as soldiers. Much may be presented in
favor of his "offensive-defensive" concept as well-suited to the
states' rights attitudes of southerners. And his judgment regarding a departmental command system, later expanded into
something of a theater command system, anticipated related
developments by the United States during World War II. A
big negative point is contained in the charge that Davis insisted on running military operations himself. Primarily an
adviser to the president, Bragg was not a general-in-chief in
the sense that Grant became Lincoln's general-in-chief. Only
within a few weeks of its collapse did the Confederacy create
such a position. And then it was too late to test its utility.

Of all the complaints against Davis, none has been projected
more often than the political failing that he did not get along
well with the Confederate Congress, with several influential
southern governors, or with Vice President Alexander H.

Stephens. Blame for the friction with Stephens, or for Davis's chain of troubles with Georgia's Joseph E. Brown and North Carolina's Zebulon B. Vance, probably should not be laid at the president's door, for he was far more sinned against than sinning. But Davis assuredly could have performed with greater deftness, patience, and success in his congressional relationships. Eloquent when addressing crowds of citizens, and capable of warmth and magnetism in man-to-man contacts or within small groups, Davis appeared to poorest advantage in state papers addressed to the Confederate Congress and in dealing with many representatives and senators. This may have been due to an assumption on Davis's part that there was no need to cajole congressmen, with oratorical or other tricks or glosses, into doing what their minds and hearts should have told them was the right thing to do—a perilous assumption for any chief executive!

It is nearly always easier to discover flaws in a loser than in a winner. This is particularly true when the man who won was the revered, patriarchal Lincoln. Still it should be recalled that during the Civil War Davis was not the only occupant of a presidential office who committed mistakes.

Lincoln made some terribly poor choices, especially in regard to the politicians—utterly unqualified to lead troops—whom he often plucked from civil life and entrusted with brigadier-generalships. Even more unfortunate were Lincoln's selections of Ambrose E. Burnside and Joseph Hooker to head the Army of the Potomac. Nathaniel P. Banks demonstrated incapacity in the course of the Red River campaign, and there are additional examples. The day did come when Lincoln fully recognized the worth of the Grants, the Shermans, and the George H. Thomases. Such able professionals were then given the responsibilities due them. But, meanwhile, a sorry assortment of incompetents jeopardized and lost thousands of lives.

In the final year the North-South inequalities of manpower, materiel, and resources placed the Confederacy at an ever greater disadvantage. The marvel is that the South remained in the contest as long and tenaciously as it did. Somehow the southern people endured forty-eight months of hardship and horror. True, they were fighting for home and fireside against infinitely more powerful invaders. But surely part of the credit for their heroic showing should go to the Confederate leadership.

What of the personality of Davis, first as the South's provisional president and then when he headed her "permanent" government? He has been portrayed as too stiff an official, too inflexible a decision-maker, and deficient in the graces that tended to make Lincoln lovable even when engaged in the business of directing organized slaughter. Davis was "cold"— his "coldness" the more frigid when compared with Lincoln's warming glow; such is the stereotyped Jefferson Davis.

Yet there is proof in his earlier years that Davis was not cold at all. During much of the war he suffered from what was called neuralgia. Anyone who has experienced neuralgic pain is aware that being sunny and warm and consistently friendly while undergoing that type of torture is exceedingly difficult. But the neuralgia was not constant. There were many days and weeks of relief. And numerous witnesses have testified that resilience (rather than stiffness) and a willingness to consider conflicting opinions (instead of an inflexible attitude) characterized Davis time and again.

When the Confederacy lost, its president tried to avoid capture. He failed. Again we have a caricature: " Jeff Davis wearing women's clothes" when taken prisoner by the Yankees. He did have a shawl around his shoulders, but the "hoop skirt" and other figments of fiction—nothing of the sort. Davis then was committed to prison, remained there many months, and long was subjected to indignities and even cruelties under which the body and spirit of a less courageous soul would have collapsed.

Davis did not collapse. Bruised, he was not broken, but lived twenty-four years after his southland laid down its weapons. Spending a short period in Canada, he went to Europe five times—part of his purpose being to find a business position with a British firm in America. Frustrated on this score, and virtually without funds, he accepted the presidency of a Memphis insurance company which failed through no fault of his own. Now and then in his last years, he made public appearances in the South and was greeted with respect and applause and emotional tributes by those whose leader he had been. He also traveled as far west as Colorado and twice visited his Kentucky birthplace. Davis was eighty-one years old when the end came peacefully in New Orleans on December 6, 1889.

There is something about dying at the peak of a crisis that has the effect, in the cases of many historic figures, of lengthening statures and enhancing reputations. This was not the case with Taylor because the 1850 crisis had not developed all the way to belligerency that steamy summer. Taylor, too, did not die at an assassin's hand, but rather from natural causes. All the circumstances surrounding Lincoln's death were different. Here was the victor, here the hero of the greatest war, here the "Father Abraham" of the boys in blue, shot without warning by a Confederate sympathizer at the zenith of the Union's success. The first presidential assassination, the killing of Lincoln inspired eulogists to extol the martyred chieftain in city after city and town after town. Amid unprecedented sable pageantry, Lincoln the president was apotheosized—and Lincoln the man likewise.

No such special setting or unusual circumstance attended the death of Davis. It might be supposed that he "had lived too long" to be remembered, and that his passing in his eighty-second year would seem but an incident in men's minds. Yet to New Orleans, people came by the thousands to gaze on Davis's classic features for the final time and to attend his funeral service.

Throughout the South, from Virginia to Texas, bells tolled and minute guns were fired; and in church and assembly hall and mansion and cottage, deep and pervading grief was felt. Messages of consolation then reached, and later continued to reach, the widow from large numbers of sympathizers including her husband's former slaves. A gray-bearded college friend from the Transylvania days who had served with the deceased in the United States Senate journeyed to the Crescent City from a far-off northern place and stood tearfully among the bereaved. The last surviving member of Davis's West Point class likewise was among those present. Fourteen of the fifty pallbearers were Confederate generals. And the vast assemblage of other mourners—at least fifty thousand of them—bore mute testimony to the esteem in which Davis was held by fellow southerners. Never in the annals of the South had a funeral been so largely attended.

"Jefferson Davis," declared the *New York Times*, "will live longer in history and better than will any who have ever spoken against him." "He was the chosen chieftain," said the *New York World*, "of the new Republic which strove to establish itself, and whose adherents battled for its existence with a heroism the memory of which is everywhere cherished as one that does honor to the American character and name. . . . He sacrificed all for the cause he cherished, and he alone of all the South has borne the cross of martyrdom."

6

SLAVERY, EXTENSION, AND THE FEDERAL UNION

IN NORTHERN PORTIONS of the United States before, during, and after the Civil War, propagandists fostered the impression that an insidious "Slave Power" brought on the conflict and did so for the purpose of perpetuating the South's "peculiar institution." At best, this was an oversimplification of an extremely complex congeries of issues. Indeed, a strong case can be made that there never was a monolithic "Slave Power." And, even if one rejects the denial in a debate over definitions of terms, it is certain that numerous factors besides activities of slavery proponents figured prominently among the reasons for the four years of fighting under Lincoln and Davis.

This view is not tantamount to dismissing slavery as a major cause of the Civil War. No matter what southern congressmen might aver, and no matter what the Supreme Court might hold, ownership and control of one human being by another seemed to many people then—as they still seem today—utterly incompatible with American fundamentals. Thus many citizens became antislavery. And to that segment of those disapproving of slavery known as abolitionists, antislavery essentially was a moral cause transcending constitutional considerations and most other political concerns. Slavery was sin, said abolitionists, who (as their name indicated) sought with every means at their disposal to abolish that sin.

There was an essential difference, however, between abolitionists on one hand and most northern citizens on the other. To nearly all northerners, as well as southerners, a highly important guiding fact was the Constitution's protection of slavery in fifteen states of the federal Union. This enormous majority, utterly unlike the relatively few abolitionists, respected constitutionality and even as late as 1860 made no move to abolish slavery in the states where it was legal.

While the 1819–21 Missouri Controversy was, in Thomas Jefferson's words, a "firebell in the night," from 1822 through 1844 other issues attracted more attention than slavery in the political arena. But after the annexation of Texas and during and after the Mexican War large numbers of northern politicians and voters embraced a cause related to abolitionism, though in no sense synonymous with it. This was the cause of opposition to the *extension* of slavery.

In the post-1845 period, the antiextension drive first concentrated on the western and southwestern lands acquired from Mexico in 1848. Secondly, it shifted to that part of the soil obtained in the Louisiana Purchase and involved in the repeal of the Missouri Compromise. Initially adherents of the Free Soil party and then those of the far larger Republican party made slavery's containment within fifteen states the number-one plank of quadrennial platforms. This was the principal public issue in the congressional debates of 1850, in the Kansas-Nebraska embroilment of 1854, and in the 1860 election that brought Abraham Lincoln into the White House.

Unlike Lincoln or Zachary Taylor, Jefferson Davis had an opportunity to discuss the Civil War's causation long after hostilities ended. In *The Rise and Fall of the Confederate Government*, he traced points of agreement and difference between South and North from the era of the Declaration of Independence all the way to the firing on Fort Sumter.

The essence of Davis's statement was that "each of the

States, as sovereign parties to the compact of Union, had the reserved power to secede from it whenever it should be found not to answer the ends for which it [the Union] was established." What were those ends? They prominently included the "unalienable rights of man," the "sovereignty of the people," and the "supremacy of law." All these were predicated upon man's prior allegiance to his state, vis-à-vis the United States, which in Davis's view definitely was not the sovereign. "The temper of the Black Republicans is not to give us our rights in the Union, or allow us to go peaceably out of it," he wrote on January 13, 1861. "If we had no other cause, this would be enough to justify secession, at whatever hazard." This still was Davis's opinion when death came to him nearly twenty-nine years later.

In *The Rise and Fall* Davis likewise said that, in various North-South relationships over a span of seven decades from the 1770s to the 1840s, the "existence of African servitude" was in no wise a cause of conflict, but "only an incident." In subsequent controversies, however, slavery's "effect in operating as a lever upon the passions, prejudices, or sympathies of mankind . . . was so potent that it has been spread, like a thick cloud, over the whole horizon of historic truth." In his own words, therefore, although in a roundabout way, Davis admitted that slavery was a factor in the 1861–65 denouement. Omitted from the Davis assertion is the truth that, if slavery had not existed, there would have been no controversy over its extension. In the sense of acknowledging extension or containment as the most evident question in men's thoughts and actions, we find ourselves recognizing the institution of slavery per se as an undeniable cause of war.

But slavery was not the sole reason for the four-year struggle. Among the many other causes were the pride, zeal, and hatred felt by many northerners and southerners as Armageddon approached. There undoubtedly was much intolerance from Maine to Texas and from Florida to Minnesota. Economic, cultural, philosophical, and psychological considerations were not negligible. The publication of *Uncle Tom's*

Cabin, the lies and truths and exaggerations emanating from "Bleeding" Kansas (regarding which ink flowed more freely than blood), the shrillness of speeches in and out of Congress, and the "martyrdom" of John Brown all contributed to an atmosphere of emotional excess. Some northerners had fantastic notions of the slave-labor system. Some southerners supposed the North would not fight successfully, if at all, in the event of secession. Thus fateful forms of ignorance were present on both sides of the Mason-Dixon Line.

A great deal may be said in favor of Davis's constitutional credo, which was also the basic belief of many of his fellow southern leaders. But, examining the situation in practical rather than theoretical terms, it is also permissible to speculate—over a century after the killing and being killed—whether southern interest might not have retained much protection if the South had remained in the Union.

Slavery was not seen as the only southern interest. It is probable that, even with full southern delegations seated in Congress, a heavily protective tariff would have been enacted and signed into law, benefiting the manufacturing North to the disadvantage of the agricultural South. With ever-increasing majorities in both the Senate and the House, northerners also could have imposed other legislation detrimental to southerners.

Yet, with a very large and ever-vocal and alert minority representing southern wishes on Capitol Hill, it is extremely doubtful that anything resembling total northern dominance would have developed prior to the passing of many decades. It ought to be realized, too, that the Democratic party would have remained a national party—and, in all probability, the only national party—for a long time. Even after the Civil War and despite conditions of Reconstruction voting, the Republican nominee in 1868 managed to win the presidency against a weak Democratic opponent by only a tiny popular margin. In 1876, 1880, 1884, 1888, and 1892, history records that post-Civil War Democratic candidates performed creditably in the era of the bloody shirt. And, concurrently, Democratic congressional strength proved impressive. What might the South have achieved, within the Democratic fold, if men like Davis had been willing to theorize less and calculate more?

What might have been the ultimate fate of slavery in such circumstances? Scholars have debated how profitable it was in the states where it was legal, and also whether it would have been profitable in various regions of the West. If southern commonwealths had not seceded, slavery would have continued there for a time. How long, nobody knows. The author's opinion is that it would have been eliminated around the turn of the century, probably with considerable fuss but without slaughter a la 1861–65. Someone else may think differently. But, regardless of slavery's fate and in the light of points made in the preceding paragraph, it appears certain that the South would have fared better from the 1860s to the 1890s if the Confederacy had never been created.

Still another telling consideration regarding southern power within the federal government has to do with congressional committees in the last third of the nineteenth century and the first two-thirds of the twentieth century. We all know that, starting in the 1870s and 1880s, the South reaped a variety of advantages by keeping House and Senate members in Congress for long spans of time. One result was that, during those periods when Democrats possessed Senate and House majorities, most congressional committees were chaired by southerners. And when Republican majorities prevailed, the ranking members of committee minorities similarly hailed from the South and made their influence felt. It is not farfetched to say that, if secession was the most serious misstep southerners made, their exploitation of the seniority system on Capitol Hill was most representative of southern shrewdness. As this quest for disproportionate southern power turned out to be achievable despite the outcome of the Civil War, might it not have worked to even more spectacular advantage without a Sumter or an Appomattox?

Hindsight strongly suggests that both Abraham Lincoln and Zachary Taylor were more practical men than Jefferson Davis. By northern consolidated-state standards, they were Unionists

—and therefore patriots—and he was not. Davis, nevertheless, would forever deny any doubts about his devotion to the Union as he interpreted the Union. Throughout the Civil War, he and like-minded southerners customarily avoided the word Union when referring to the adversary government or to adversary armies. He believed in a Union with a right of secession. Long after relinquishing the Confederate presidency, he wrote, "I recognize the fact that the war showed . . . secession . . . to be impracticable, but this did not prove it to be wrong."

Abraham Lincoln today is considered America's greatest president both in scholarly circles and by the general public. Assuredly, he merits lofty rank. What many moderns forget, however, is that in the 1840s Lincoln said, "Any people anywhere being inclined and having the power have the right to rise up and shake off the existing government, and form one that suits them better." He said nothing of the sort in 1860 or 1861. In 1858, Lincoln declared that he was not "in favor of bringing about in any way the social and political equality of the white and black races." To what extent does that statement accord with the convictions of some of his modern admirers? In 1860, Lincoln opposed inclusion of an anti-Fugitive Slave Law plank in the Republican platform—and in line with his wishes the plank was excluded. This is interesting in light of the emphasis placed on the law's iniquities by many antislavery persons. On his journey to Washington in 1861, the president-elect told audience after audience that peace would not give way to war. Did Lincoln believe what he repeatedly asserted? There is no strong evidence to the contrary. Yet before long, as President, he was writing, "The tug of war has to come, and better now than at any time hereafter."

In the totality of Lincoln's expressions prior to the firing on Fort Sumter, there is nothing like the degree of consistency found in the totality of Davis's expressions. Was Davis's consistency foolish, reminiscent of the Emersonian adage that "A foolish consistency is the hobgoblin of little minds . . ."? Surely, only a cynic would think so. But, as we have seen, the bulk of Lincoln's reputation rests upon his post-Sumter, not his pre-Sumter, record. If the problems he faced in the presidential chair were by no means as enormous as those Davis confronted, Lincoln certainly met and mastered them. His mistakes proved incidental in the long run. Time and time again, in challenge after challenge, he demonstrated extraordinarily sound judgment both in his relations with Congress and the public and in his role as commander-in-chief.

Yet soundness of judgment alone was not enough to lift Lincoln to the heights of popular esteem. Having the asset of an unusual personality, he managed, without the advantages of television or radio, to project his individualistic image to the northern populace as a whole. His common sense, decency, seeming simplicity, and anecdotal glosses on complex topics not only reached fellow Americans, but also sold and resold men and women on the proposition that he was the right person for his power and place. A few of his predecessors and successors have rivaled Lincoln on this score, but no other president has surpassed him—and it is doubtful that any has been his equal—on a sustained basis.

Appealing to, gaining, and then retaining the support and devotion of so substantial a constituency, Lincoln had two types of assets in his dealings with members of Congress. First, he was already clothed with presidential authority— including patronage power, which was bound to be far more awesome in wartime than amid scenes of peace. At least equally consequential, senators and representatives knew that Lincoln (unlike Pierce and Buchanan) was sustained by the people, and that to oppose him meant running a risk of incurring popular resentment. Lincoln, moreover, often was anticipatory. This may be considered a third major asset, for repeatedly he gave evidence that his sense of timing could be letter perfect. Possessing sizable advantages over Davis to start with, Lincoln knew how to make the most of them. Thus, capitalizing on conditions that favored him, he skirted the bogs and quicksands of dissension and led the nation to victory.

History teachers are aware how easy it is to rivet students' attention on colorful events—wars, revolutions, and the like—and how hard to arouse comparable interest in long-range causes of dramatic developments. The inceptions of problems, the ifs and might-have-beens, often fail to make an impact on students, even when the material is presented with skill. This generalization applies to adult, as well as youthful, minds. And an excellent example of the fact exists in the America of the 1970s in the contrast between most citizens' knowledge of the Civil War and their ignorance concerning the war's antecedents.

Because no war came in 1850, the crisis of that year arouses few emotions, inspires few thoughts, and is a blur in too many brains. The historically discredited concept of a nonexistent "Clay Compromise" remains a widely accepted stereotype. Despite the activities of Henry Clay in the spotlight on Capitol Hill, there was no Whig compromise and there was no "Clay Compromise," and any person professing the contrary is unfamiliar with what occurred. While Clay and his fellow congressional Whigs did contribute to the 1850 adjustment, the compromise was essentially a Democratic one—with the Clay-Whig contributions merely supplemental.

If most moderns fail to grasp such fundamentals, what hope is there that they will comprehend Zachary Taylor's significant role in the 1850 setting? Taylor was one of only 1,800 southerners owning as many as a hundred slaves. Thus did he not belong to what might be considered a socioeconomic southern elite or, in current jargon, the "southern establishment"? Had there been a monolithic "Slave Power," surely Taylor's investments in plantations and slaves qualified him to be part of that power. As president of the United States, was not this well-to-do planter and slaveholder in a position to work and scheme to great effect in accordance with the aims of so many of his class?

Instead of fitting neatly into such a stereotype, Zachary Taylor did just the opposite. Instead of contributing to the alleged endeavors of the nonexistent "Slave Power," he committed his administration to the containment of slavery. He did not do so through any declared approval of the Wilmot Proviso, which explicitly called for slavery's exclusion from the West and Southwest. But, unquestionably, the desired end product of Taylor's policy and actions was identical with the goal of the Proviso's supporters. Lincoln was one of Taylor's contemporaries who understood what was going on. If that had not been the case, it is inconceivable that Lincoln would have lauded Taylor in the language penned for delivery at Chicago's city hall.

When all except two northern Whigs in the Senate lined up in support of Taylor's plan, and when numerous northern Whigs in the House did the same, the president's position as an antiextension leader was clearly observable. Then Taylor died. His fellow Whig, Fillmore, adopted a diametrically contrary stand so far as compromising was concerned. Stephen A. Douglas, Democrat from Illinois, emerged from the wings of the congressional stage. Douglas and his fellow Democrats—aided by the Whigs Clay, Fillmore, and Webster, but not by the Democrat Davis—pushed the Compromise of 1850 through the Senate and the House. Thus they substantially reduced the immediate prospect of civil strife.

It is highly probable that, had Taylor lived, his blunt Lincoln-like nationalism would have triumphed over any Texas sortie against Santa Fe and would have defeated any other challenge to United States authority. Some historians have set forth their beliefs in the logic of such a development. According to James Schouler, Taylor "saw more clearly the bold headlands of national policy . . . than the wisest and world-renowned of our statesmen." Edward Channing agreed: "It seems not impossible that . . . Taylor . . . had more political prescience than the most veteran political war horses of them all." George Fort Milton believed, "The stern determined character of 'Old Rough and Ready' made it more than likely that the revolt would not have gotten so far and taken so long as the Civil War itself."

Some later writers have disagreed, prominent among them Allan Nevins who characterized Taylor as "wrongheaded." If Taylor was wrongheaded in 1850, one may respectfully inquire, how could Lincoln have been so rightheaded in 1861? Did economic, social, or political changes between those two

critical years override in importance the similarities in principle of Taylor's and Lincoln's nationalism?

In the South, of course, Taylor became very unpopular during his presidential months. Deceased, he remained unpopular there. Most antiextension people in the North, moreover,
failed to make a hero of him in the years following his death.
Why? Because, as they grew increasingly critical of the South
as a whole, they could not equate the attitude and action of the
Louisiana-Mississippi slaveholder with the cherished "Slave
Power" fiction. So it was that, had it not been for a few scholars
who brushed aside propaganda mists and uncovered realities,
the twelfth president would have remained forever in a historical no-man's-land claimed by neither South nor North.

To no such extent has either Davis or Lincoln ever been a
candidate for limbo or obscurity. A plausible case may be
made that the relationships of the two Civil War presidents to
other state and regional influences—as well as to Kentucky
associations—have appeared to readers of their biographies to
account largely for their prewar and wartime postures. For
example, it is sensible to think that eight years of Mississippi
isolation and study and the exclusive intellectual companion-
ship of his brother turned Davis away from Kentucky—and
from northwestern-oriented westernness—in the direction of
the southernness he ultimately embraced. And, surely, we
have no difficulty in finding that Lincoln's experiences in an
Indiana-Illinois environment verified and extended his Kentucky frontier westernness.

An equally important reason for the dispelling of obscurity
or confusion about Lincoln and Davis is that the historio-
graphic focus on the Civil War has been so sharp. Succeeding
generations have not always interpreted all the 1861–65 actions and words, motivations and hopes, of Davis and Lincoln
in exactly the same way. There have been substantial scholarly
and literary divergences. Yet interest in the wartime scene has
been so constant and so keen that, in one study or another,
most fundamentals concerning the leaders have come to light.
Not so in the case of Taylor, who had been dead for over a

decade when the Civil War began and who was president in a period which has seemed far less dramatic to the public as a whole—and (probably for that reason) has been less frequently and less intensively scrutinized.

Years before he acquired Deep South land, Zachary Taylor was a nationalist to the core. He grew up in Kentucky when Kentuckians identified themselves at least as much with the West as with the South, under frontier conditions and with frontier outlooks. In his first important military achievement, he defended the Northwest against foes of the federal Union. Thereafter, for decades, his army service took him to Northwest and Southwest alike, reinforcing his boyhood westernness and making him a westerner and a nationalist through and through.

It is true that Taylor came of age in a slave state and that his father was a slaveholder. It is also true that, when young, he himself acquired slaves; and, when older, he purchased more of them.

Yet there is nothing whatever in his record to indicate that private economic interests—linked with slavery or cotton or anything else—overslaughed his devotion to the Union at any point, or dictated his stand on public questions. Economic determinists will forever have difficulty in reconciling Taylor's presidential posture, like that of Andrew Jackson regarding South Carolina, with the slightest semblance of selfishness. In Taylor, America had a Kentucky-reared chief executive who—through Jackson-like and Lincoln-like presidential Unionism—sought to avoid what his son-in-law Davis and his staunch adherent Lincoln at length became so deeply engaged in: the killing and maiming of hundreds of thousands of America's young men.

Epilogue

S OME READERS will doubtless agree that the interplay of these three personalities and what they stood for might be hard to accept as true-to-life if Lincoln, Davis, and Taylor had never existed and were presented to the public in a novel or on the stage. That history is stranger than fiction is so truistic that the assertion has long been regarded as banal. Yet rarely has a playwright or a novelist dealt with materials more replete with drama than the Lincoln-Davis-Taylor intertwinings.

Take, for instance, the mathematical odds against Davis's fighting in Mexico under the command of his former father-in-law. Consider the degree of improbability that the Brier-field anchorite would rival the general as a Buena Vista hero. Think of the mutual respect and affection of the two men in 1849–50, when they—so antipathetic in the past—disagreed completely on the country's prime issue.

Turn, then, to all the similarities (in the midst of expected dissimilarities) in the Davis-Lincoln lives before 1861, and in the triumphs, disasters, and sorrows of the southern and northern commanders in chief. Finally, reexamine the words and phrases chosen in Chicago by ex-Congressman Lincoln for the purpose of extolling Taylor. In describing Taylor's presidential record, Lincoln uncannily forecast his own.

Think, too, of the turns of history causing one of these three persons to become a Southerner with western affiliations who served as the president of the Confederacy; one of them a Westerner with southern affiliations who won election to the presidency of the United States; and one of them a kind of transcendent Westerner whom many Americans today see as the greatest of our presidents. All had roots in the western-southern Kentucky experience.

The author hopes this book will help dispel a number of half-truths and total misconceptions concerning the trio herein discussed. If that hope is realized, and if in the process the history of Kentucky and the Union is clarified, he will feel abundantly rewarded.

Bibliographical Essay

EXCELLENT BOOKS about Abraham Lincoln are so numerous that any knowledgeable historian, endeavoring to recommend the finest and most useful, will have far more qualms respecting omissions than inclusions. No treatment of the mature Lincoln is sounder than James G. Randall and Richard N. Current, *Lincoln the President*, 4 vols. (New York, 1945–53). Delightfully and even brilliantly written is Carl Sandburg, *Abraham Lincoln: The War Years*, 4 vols. (New York, 1939). Among many creditable contributions supplementing those works are William B. Hesseltine, *Lincoln and the War Governors* (New York, 1948); T. Harry Williams, *Lincoln and the Radicals* (Madison, 1941), and Kenneth P. Williams, *Lincoln Finds a General*, 5 vols. (New York, 1949–59).

Benjamin P. Thomas, *Abraham Lincoln: A Biography* (New York, 1952), for a quarter century has been considered the best one-volume study. Henceforth it should be perused in conjunction with Stephen B. Oates, *With Malice Toward None: The Life of Abraham Lincoln* (New York, 1977); the latter is mentioned despite several slants which I regard as awry. Of high quality is Don E. Fehrenbacher, *Prelude to Greatness: Lincoln in the 1850's* (Stanford, 1962). Ruth P. Randall, *Mary Lincoln: Biography of a Marriage* (Boston, 1953), has not been wholly superseded by Justin G. Turner and Linda Levitt Turner, *Mary Todd Lincoln: Her Life and Letters* (New York, 1972). Fundamental to scholarly insights are Roy P. Basler et al., eds., *The Collected Works of Abraham Lincoln*, 9 vols. (New Brunswick, New Jersey, 1953–55), and Roy P. Basler, ed., *The Collected Works of Abraham Lincoln, Supplement, 1832–1865* (Westport, Connecticut, 1974).

Neither in the last century nor in this one have books concerning Jefferson Davis approached those about Lincoln in numbers or quality. Defects of omission or commission mar the efforts of William E. Dodd, Hamilton J. Eckenrode, Armistead C. Gordon, Robert M. McElroy, and Robert W. Winston. A far longer biography by Hudson Strode came out in the course of a decade: *Jefferson Davis: American Patriot, 1808–1861* (New York, 1955), *Jefferson Davis: Confederate President* (New York, 1959), and *Jefferson Davis: Tragic Hero, The Last Twenty-four Years, 1864–1889* (New York, 1964). Although the Strode work has attractive passages and is illuminated by much fresh material, the multiplicity of errors necessitates its being read with caution. In many ways, the most reliable account of Davis's life as a whole is Clement Eaton, *Jefferson Davis* (New York, 1977).

Writers who lacked ready access to the scattered Davis manuscripts long were forced to turn with misgivings to Dunbar Rowland, ed., *Jefferson Davis, Constitutionalist: His Letters, Papers and Speeches*, 10 vols. (Jackson, Mississippi, 1923), and to Varina Howell Davis, *Jefferson Davis, Ex-President of the Confederate States of America: A Memoir by His Wife*, 2 vols. (New York, 1890). Superior scholarship is evident in Haskell M. Monroe, Jr., and James T. McIntosh, eds., *The Papers of Jefferson Davis*, 2 vols. to date (Baton Rouge, 1971, 1974). Because Davis is carried in *The Papers* only so far as mid-1846, Rowland's *Jefferson Davis, Constitutionalist* will continue temporarily to serve a purpose, notwithstanding its deficiencies.

The most comprehensive Taylor biography was published in two parts: Holman Hamilton, *Zachary Taylor: Soldier of the Republic* (Indianapolis, 1941), and *Zachary Taylor: Soldier in the White House* (Indianapolis, 1951). Both volumes were reissued in 1966 by Archon Books, Hamden, Connecticut. They and Brainerd Dyer, *Zachary Taylor* (Baton Rouge, 1946) are products of scholarly investigation. Among other Taylor titles are Oliver O. Howard, *General Taylor* (New York, 1892), and Silas B. McKinley and Silas Bent, *Old Rough and Ready* (New

York, 1946). There has been no publication of all of Taylor's known writings. But prepresidential samples are available in William H. Sampson, ed., *Letters of Zachary Taylor from the Battlefields of the Mexican War* (Rochester, New York, 1908; reprinted New York, 1969).

Many vignettes, character assessments, and other depictions of both Lincoln and Davis appear in histories of the Civil War. Most trustworthy on that subject is James G. Randall and David Donald, *The Civil War and Reconstruction*, rev. ed. (New York, 1969). Also recommended are Bruce Catton, *The Centennial History of the Civil War*, 3 vols. (Garden City, New York, 1961–65); Shelby Foote, *The Civil War: A Narrative History*, 3 vols. (New York, 1958–74); David Donald, ed., *Why the North Won the Civil War* (Baton Rouge, 1960); Frank E. Vandiver, *Rebel Brass: The Confederate Command System* (Baton Rouge, 1956), and "Jefferson Davis—Leader without Legend," *Journal of Southern History* 43 (February 1977): 3–18; and William and Bruce Catton, *Two Roads to Sumter* (New York, 1963).

Justin H. Smith, *The War with Mexico*, 2 vols. (New York, 1919) long was regarded as outstanding on that subject, but since the 1940s it has been subjected to telling criticism. It won both the Pulitzer and Loubat prizes and was reprinted in Gloucester, Massachusetts, in 1963. Briefer and less vulnerable coverage is to be found in Robert S. Henry, *The Story of the Mexican War* (Indianapolis, 1950); in Otis A. Singletary, *The Mexican War* (Chicago, 1960); and in Seymour V. Connor and Odie B. Faulk, *North America Divided: The Mexican War, 1846–1848* (New York, 1971). All these contain data on, and estimates of, Zachary Taylor as a man and a general, as does Edward J. Nichols, *Zach Taylor's Little Army* (New York, 1963).

Holman Hamilton, *Prologue to Conflict: The Crisis and Compromise of 1850* (Lexington, Kentucky, 1964) is a detailed treatment of that topic. A paperback edition was issued in New York in 1966. Allan Nevins produced a multivolume work on America from 1847 to 1865. The overall title is *Ordeal of the Union*, 8 vols. (New York, 1948–71). Involved here is something of a bibliographical nightmare as *Ordeal of the Union* is likewise the title of Nevins's first two volumes which cover 1847–57; *The Emergence of Lincoln* treats 1857–61, and *The War for the Union* deals with 1861–65. Roy F. Nichols, *The Disruption of American Democracy* (New York, 1948) should certainly be consulted for the years immediately preceding the Lincoln-Davis presidencies. And the outstanding work on the entire period between the Mexican and Civil Wars is David M. Potter (with Don E. Fehrenbacher), *The Impending Crisis, 1848–1861* (New York, 1976).

Closeup analyses of all national political campaigns in which Lincoln, Davis, and Taylor were involved are in volumes 1 and 2 of Arthur M. Schlesinger, Jr., and Fred L. Israel, eds., *History of American Presidential Elections, 1789–1968*, 4 vols. (New York, 1971). Oddly, however, the highly important 1860 election is discussed in the Schlesinger-Israel work less satisfactorily than are the other pertinent contests.